Does
Therapy
Work?

Jane Barclay

Troutbeck Press

First published in 2011
by Troutbeck Press
Copyright © 2011 Jane Barclay
www.jbcounselling.co.uk

Front cover artwork by John Cooper
Exeter, Devon

Book design by Momentum Graphics
www.momentumgraphics.co.uk

Printed by imprintdigital.net
Inside pages on 100% recycled paper.

Orders: Troutbeck Press
PO Box 747, Exeter EX1 9RS
admin@troutbeckpress.co.uk
www.jbcounselling.co.uk

ISBN: 978-0-9567857-0-1

DOES THERAPY WORK?

Jane Barclay practises as a Therapeutic Counsellor in Exeter, Devon. She also works with clients on behalf of GamCare (www.gamcare.org.uk).

She is a member of The Association of Humanistic Psychology Practitioners (www.ahpp.org).

From 2002–2003 she wrote the regular column for the journal Self & Society, A Forum for Contemporary Psychology (published by The Association for Humanistic Psychology in Britain). Titles include: *To smack or not to smack, Room for Both, Heroes & Villains, The Power of Remorse.*

Articles also published in Self & Society: *Class, Prejudice and Privilege* (2002), *'I can't get no-o… Satisfaction'* (2004), *Sacrifice* (2007).

Published in Attachment: New Directions in Psychotherapy and Relational Psychoanalysis (Karnac Press): *Endings, to have and to hold* (2010).

Published by Boarding Concern (www.boardingconcern.org.uk): *The Trauma of Boarding at School* (2010).

ACKNOWLEDGEMENTS

I thank all my teachers: my tutors in Therapeutic Counselling; each therapist I have worked with and each supervisor; the members of my training groups; the members of my ongoing peer supervision group; and each client I have worked with.

I thank Alison, Angela, Annie, Di, Jane, Jane, Pippa, Prue and Stefan for support at different times. And the Samaritans.

I thank Sally, my writing mentor.

And I thank Iain, for recognising more of me before I did, and for being alongside me through to completion of 'Does Therapy Work?'

To my children

γνῶθι σεαυτόν

gnōthi seauton

(know thyself)

Socrates

CONTENTS

INTRODUCTION

'Does therapy work?'

The question was fired at me late one evening at a party. I started. I had no succinct answer. By the time I'd taken a breath, the conversation had moved on.

I awoke the next morning humming with energy to put my own work as therapist under the microscope. First, what did my scientist friend mean by 'work'? What was this thing called therapy? What exactly happened? How? What was my part?

Twelve years ago, as a student of therapeutic counselling, I became a client in therapy myself. I wrote from the start, both accounts of sessions and the jumble of emotions, sensations and thoughts in between. Recognising the value of firsthand experience, I turned my scribbled notes into a case-study of myself to present as part of my diploma. But I didn't stop there; writing had become my lifeline. I clung to the part of me who was able to remain curious, observing and recording my experiences as I navigated a way through. I've drawn deeply from these earlier writings.

For the scornful ('self-indulgent navel-gazing') and suspicious ('exploitative') I hope my book at least evokes interest. I've written of human relationships in terms broader than biological functions and chemical interactions but avoided therapy-speak. I've examined and evaluated the work of therapy which resists precise measurement. I've discovered both the limitations of language and the border where proof tussles with belief. It is my desire for clarity *and* love of mystery, my hunger to know *and* admiration for that which eludes definition that have fuelled me to write about a practice which is essentially creative, from whichever perspective.

If therapy is to be more widely respected and valued as a response to both acute and chronic distress and offered alongside our mainstream medical model of care, fuller awareness and deeper understanding is vital. I'm hugely grateful to my friend for his question, from which has grown this very considered reply.

PART ONE

Examination

CHAPTER ONE

THE COMPONENT PARTS

(Faced with the usual dilemma about pronouns, I've chosen to use 'he' for the client and 'she' for the therapist. When I use 'we' I speak for collective attitudes, actions and instincts as I perceive them; I do not assume to know anyone else's personal experiences or to reflect individual beliefs.)

First, the client. A human being of any race, culture, class, sexual orientation. A person developed and continually developing from a mixture of genetic encoding, cultural inheritance and experiences in both the immediate and wider environment continually sensed through nose, mouth, ears, eyes, and skin – the information received being processed via intricate chemical and electrical activity in the brain to inform choices and shape character. A person whose instinct is to promote survival, born with the means to respond if threatened by mobilising Fight/Flight energy or by Freezing this energy (see Chapter Two); whose words, behaviour and demeanour make up a language to connect with others, also to serve survival. Someone who responds to a call within himself to seek contact (directly or via symptomatic expressions of anguish) with another human for whom he has no personal responsibility, hoping this contact will ease distress whatever its source.

The client may seek help from a therapist as a last resort, having tried medication to numb or escape emotional pain, or self-medicated. He may come in response to an immediate crisis; he may call after prolonged procrastination, doubtful and suspicious but desperate; or, maybe, make contact after measured deliberation. He will most probably be, to some extent, wary; curious perhaps, too; likely in some measure to feel ashamed of needing help, scared of neediness being exposed, of being vulnerable. He most probably wants something to change, in himself, in someone else or in outside circumstances, current or past – even though he knows the latter isn't possible.

He may well hope the therapist can work some magic, especially where all other tactics have failed, to dispel feelings that are painful and therefore unwelcome, often termed 'negative': rage, jealousy, grief, shame, despair. Or to curtail self-sabotaging compulsions, including addictions.

In our culture, professionals – teachers, doctors, lawyers, therapists – are generally regarded as experts, and as such are expected to fix, mend or adjust whatever doesn't work well for us.

Next, the human who responds to the client's call. The therapist is all of the above, with the addition of formal training. This may or may not include the experience of in-depth therapy herself over a substantial period.

There is continued dispute among training organisations and accrediting bodies as well as trainees and practitioners over the requirement to be a client in therapy, the argument being that if therapy is not sought voluntarily the work is rendered meaningless. I maintain that if the training is selected voluntarily and therapy is a course requirement, the choice is made at the outset.

Only by experiencing the position of client can a therapist know, fully enough to practice ethically, how the dynamic of this relationship differs from any other. Just as every parent has been a child, and the way we parent our own children is hugely shaped and informed by the way we were parented (see Appendix, *The Child, the Family and the Outside World*), to which we add role-models such as relations and teachers, so the therapist learns more by absorption than instruction (the difference between being shown and being told) from being client.

My own experience as client of being vulnerable, needy and at times ashamed helps me meet the mistrust with which in varying degrees each client approaches relationship with me. Crucially, being a client also does away with the 'us' and 'them' dynamic which can bring a false sense of superiority ('I'm alright, Jack') to the relationship which by its nature carries an imbalance of power.

What are the qualities a therapist learns through training and personal therapy, and continually practises? Indeed, can qualities, as well as skills, be acquired and practised or are they inherent? And what differs from being a friend or partner, however caring and attentive a listener?

As therapist, I work to practise being with someone as he reveals his experience *without making it my own*. Being alongside someone else and imagining his experience as if it were mine without getting lost in it, allows for true moments of empathy: an understanding far beyond the intellectual alone, a felt-with-the-senses understanding and appreciation. This ability relies on my therapist having been with me this way, tolerating my feelings so I can tolerate my own rather than follow the fear-based path of trying to avoid or change them.

When an experience occurs brains become wired a particular way, neural pathways are formed between nerve cells. Through repetition we form habits, as connections between neurons (nerve cells) travel along already-used pathways. We become familiar with what we know. Hence we are drawn to similar experiences, painful ones as well as joyful, however much our rational selves may argue and will-power attempts to resist. New experiences bring awareness of neurotransmitters' chemical release or electrical charge (accompanied by interest, excitement, anxiety or, if extreme enough, a flooding rush,) that connects via synapses from neurons 'a' to receptors in neurons 'b'. No wonder clients' initial fight against feeling feelings and receiving comfort if these practices are new. Compare brain *un*learning and *re*wiring with breaking and resetting your nose: however much you may want the end result, aren't you bound to hesitate, feel discomfort, and take a while to become familiar with the new look and feel?

Presence of another person, who neither invades nor remains aloof but works to maintain appropriate distance moment by moment, is above all else the enabling factor that encourages the client to become aware of and experience himself, feelings included, more fully, and promotes the growth of resources to support the regaining of balance (see Chapter Two).

As therapist I need patience too, which also requires practice. For a client to develop enough trust in me to let in care and support is, like all brain-rewiring, likely to be a bumpy ride and take time. Too much disclosure too quickly may be followed by reactive shying away. Arriving late, missing an appointment or filling a session with distracting anecdotes: these and more are clues that the speed and depth are agitating rather than soothing debilitating panic. From the first meeting, therefore, the core issue is safety in terms of balancing needs both for contact and for ability to self-protect.

Practising being present with my client and his experience has meant recognising, challenging and working with my own, hard-wired desire to escape feelings; has meant tolerating discomfort that arises from doing something differently. Recognising that a momentary urge to rush through or leap a client's feelings comes from reluctance to connect with my own, helps: having this awareness helps me separate my client's story and feelings from mine, helps me be with his and park mine for attention later. What confuses the issue is the possibility that I may, by instinctively mirroring my client and being open to his experience, be unable to distinguish both his reluctance and impatience from my own (see Appendix, *Help for the Helper*). Reconnection to old, discarded habits requires ongoing vigilance.

The more a client side-tracks the discomfort stage and focuses exclusively on behaving differently (on 'getting there'), the more change depends upon reason and the effort of conscious willpower. Which brings me back to being therapist: if I cannot be with how I am, how can I be with how someone else is? If I cannot tolerate my own distress hearing someone's story, how can I make space for and tolerate, indeed welcome, his?

Intent to change is a wonderful energy. Rewiring that endures cannot be hurried or forced; change of any magnitude involves taking risks small enough to bear, big enough to appreciate; depends upon practising; and upon having support, encouragement and witness from another person.

I understand the incremental process of integration in terms of re-membering, of locating and joining up parts of the self, each vital and valuable, including 'negative' feelings (since the term 'negative' carries judgement together with the desire to rid, I prefer the term 'shadow'), which have become detached, all contributing to the uncomfortable sense of 'something's missing'. In extreme form, this can be experienced as a gaping hole, a void – indicating shock of some kind.

The neuroscience that supports this process is based on research into trauma (experienced as threat to existence of self and/or others) that tracks chemical changes during the Fight/ Flight response (including release by neurotransmitters of adrenalin and cortisol to increase heart-rate and close down the digestive system), and the return to equilibrium (the activities of the parasympathetic branch of the Autonomic Nervous System) when, and only when, danger is passed or survived (see Appendix, *The Body Remembers*). Animals seem to recover naturally. As well as checking out the surrounding environment, humans seem to need to tell the story to have it witnessed in order to confirm that the event really is over (I suspect pack animals seek reassurance too, by huddling within their herd), yet resist this process since it involves another human. Therein lies the conflict: the need for and resistance to contact. On our own we struggle to discharge the residual energy that animals simply shake out (see Appendix, *Waking the Tiger*). Without physical and emotional release, we continue to live in a state of red-alert, 'as if', which inevitably inhibits relaxed functioning (sleep, digestion, sexual arousal), let alone enjoyment.

To recover from the Freeze response to trauma is challenging. An animal freezes when it's doomed to be eaten, or trapped, doomed to die. Its system shuts down to reduce pain. If it isn't eaten (perhaps its predator is distracted), or is somehow released, it will in its own time come round to full consciousness. Humans who don't 'come round' once danger is passed, and the ones who are actually trapped for an indeterminate period (children neglected, hit, and sexually violated; hostages; prisoners of war), maintain the 'startle' position (the sympathetic branch of the Autonomic Nervous System continuing to pump 'stress' hormones) until release comes – no wonder waiting (in a traffic jam, for a train or simply meeting a friend for coffee) can trigger extreme stress.

The devices formed to manage ongoing tension become hard-wired, often normalised to the point of being unnoticed – including mistrust of fellow humans.

Consider veterans and prisoners of war of the past hundred years who, wanting to leave it all behind, never told; and the servicemen and women today who still don't, from inhibition and from lack of opportunity. Consider the fallout from this silence in the form of illness, stresses and addictions as the traumatised part of each one remains locked away to struggle alone, ignored; consider the loss to themselves, to their children and children's children.

In my darkest times as client, I wanted my therapist to do more than listen, witness and empathise with my story. I wanted him to take it, and my terror that escalated as I told, away. I remembered, suddenly, the distinct moment, aged seven, when I gazed across the lawn from my family's front door thinking, 'Only me, no one else, sees what I see out of my eyes.' Objectively interesting as that observation had been then, it now evoked desolation. Hence my desire for my therapist not just to appreciate how I felt but also to make me better by feeling it for me. Even after I worked out that if he was terrified too I'd be no safer, I persistently tried.

What I learned, even while I hated and raged at him for holding his separateness rather than be sucked in, was the power that came from the supportive presence of another person. This came about gradually, for only gradually dared I let in his care.

Once I had begun to register my therapist's close-but-distinct presence through a gradual process of relaxing my guard, the feelings I was remembering that I understood to belong to other times, became more knowable as mine alone, more bearable, and survivable. I began to trust they wouldn't kill me; the internal relationship between me and my emotions was rebalancing.

How else, without being client myself, could I have gained enough personal awareness of my feelings and needs necessary to protect the relationships I was going to enter into with clients? Only with such awareness (hence the need as therapist for continuing self-enquiry), can I afford to relax guard of my self and venture into the other person's world with clear attention and no agenda to change it, on the understanding that I'm visiting, not moving in.

Emotions are contagious; as animals, we watch our herd for signals that individually we might have missed, our brain neurons copying and mapping the information we gather in through our senses. I watch a horror movie and feel fear (my face probably mirrors the ones on the screen); I lose myself in a love story, feel the grief of the abandoned party, the rage of the betrayed lover. The more the story I witness resembles my own, the stronger the identification; the more flashes spark between synapses along neural pathways already formed to confirm what I know (hence the satisfaction). The lights go on and I shake myself back into the present. I may need to discuss the story with friends then or later, to assist that return.

As therapist, I am not an audience, there to enjoy a good fright, or cry, and return home relieved of emotion I've temporarily identified with. I'm there to witness, not to be voyeur, and to provide support, all the while maintaining a sense of present time and space. I do this by feeling the ground beneath my feet, by hearing the clock ticking, by taking a sip of water, by contracting and releasing muscles in my body. If my client draws close to the point of forgetting altogether where he is, of losing all contact with me (carrying severe risk of further trauma), I instigate a break for him by similar means and teach him how to do this for himself. Together and separately, we visit and come back, re-membering piece by piece.

If I didn't maintain personal boundaries and work to distinguish between my client's feelings and my own, I might resort to ways of protecting myself that would inhibit rather than facilitate his need to speak the unspeakable and feel the hitherto unfeelable. This protection might, at high cost to the therapy, include my reluctance to bring myself fully to the relationship, feelings 'n all, my refusal to risk being vulnerable too.

Dispute over 'self-disclosure of the therapist' abounds. My wail to my therapist early on, 'It has to come from you first,' as well as being a bid for him to feel my feelings for me (for rescue), was also my instinctive recognition of the need to be shown: how could I know my feelings if I didn't see his? On his face, in his voice?

The therapist's sharing of personal details is still not the same as being a friend. Any offering must be to promote the therapy, rather than be self-serving. The therapist's off-loading, and need for support, happens somewhere else, in supervision and if needed her own therapy.

Over and over again writing this book I've checked for motive and intent to ensure my carefully chosen self-disclosures serve to demystify the practice of therapy and thereby address the original question.

In day to day encounters, I automatically, and wisely, protect myself from contagion by avoidance tactics. I might redirect the subject, offer distraction, reassure. I mean well. In fact, I'm responding to an innate tendency towards recovery and balance, my own as well as friends'. (Mood-swings, as unwelcome as the discomfort can be, might simply be the disturbance felt as the nervous system insists on searching for this balance: extreme energy followed by extreme lethargy; the higher the high, the lower the low.) Setting a limit to what I can tolerate at a given moment, although good for me, is not however always as far as my friend or partner wants to go. 'Shushing', in whatever form and however kindly delivered ('don't fuss' being the harsher sort), means the full story remains untold – hence the value of a space where no shushing is required.

By showing the client how to recognise increase in Fight/ Flight/Freeze arousal (clues of pumping adrenalin include racing heart, queasiness, change in temperature), he learns to take charge of regulating the pace of telling, of keeping himself safe. Early treatment of shell shock focused on reliving rather than re-experiencing differently and with support, hence the prevalence of retraumatisation (see Appendix, *Regeneration*).

The third working part of therapy is the environment, the physical space the therapist works in that is reflected in the personal boundaries put in place. I aim for 'safe and spacious'. Attention to safety can promote or stifle creative practice; this dilemma lies at the heart of ongoing and increasingly heated debate regarding regulation. Caution fosters fear, care reassurance. Mountaineers train, assess and pack what they need and plan a route. Thereafter, they respond to conditions and make decisions moment by moment. For the climb to be exhilarating depends upon careful preparation and ongoing attention to detail.

I've experimented with boundaries to discover what works for me and reassess what I need regularly: how much time between sessions, how many clients to see in one day, how much to charge. My attention to structure is ongoing as the way I work changes.

What I wear, what and when I eat and sleep patterns all contribute to comfort: the more of what I need is in place, the more available I am to respond to the varying needs of clients, clearer about what I want to say 'yes' to and 'no' to and when I feel unsure. Taking care of myself and sharing how, offers my client a template for self-care and for relating to others; however strong his resistance (mistrust), he is bound to absorb some of what he witnesses

Ease with responding in the moment comes from listening both to gut feeling and reasoning, of maintaining balance between the two. Experience has taught me that only thinking brings me to stalemate; in any dilemma, I hear argument for both sides, decision depends on persuasion, on bias that often contains prejudice. Instinct is the animal source of information, easily located in the gut. The body doesn't lie. Understanding its messages involves collaboration between body and mind, crucial to survival.

So to the 'engine' of therapy, the relationship that grows from the interaction between these parts.

Many therapies are designed to concentrate on tasks that focus directly on the problem presented by the client, with a specific outcome in mind and a designated time in which to achieve that end, an instructive teaching model closely affiliated to our current medical model whose goal is to eliminate suffering by alleviating symptoms.

In the therapy work I present here, whatever the client brings as being the matter is not objectified, to be eradicated or somehow fixed or solved. I relate to his dis-ease as the part of my client who has a story to tell, by whatever means possible (see Appendix, *The Divided Self*).

If integration means mending relationships between part or parts that have been shocked into silence, neglected, forgotten and/or somehow set apart to take on a life of their own (hence the problem), giving attention to each part of one person can be much like investigating the dynamics in a family.

Interest in and attention to all is vital. If the overtly troubling part has grown up to protect the most vulnerable, how unwise to work towards stripping away this defence; how likely for another difficulty to form in its place. Addictive behaviours can work just like this (see Appendix, *'I can't get no-o... Satisfaction'*). The cowering parts that lie beneath rely on protection until they are safe enough to appear more explicitly. What was once problematic (for example, obsession with food) can then relax its hold, no longer needed as protection or distraction from the more elusive source of pain (see Chapter Two).

'I've got nothing to talk about today,' a client might say. Matter solved? Time to finish? An opportunity to see which lesser-known part might dare peek out and take a little of this space for itself, which voice might speak? I understand these moments, discomfort included, as ones of deepening trust (which is indeed change): no agenda, less urgent need to control the hour by packing it full. A 'let's see where we go' approach can lead to unexpected and valuable discoveries, not least the challenge of not-knowing and not-planning, of loosening control of feelings.

This form of therapy may seem a luxury, costing time and money that many say is unaffordable. I hear, and appreciate, the hesitance to engage in relationship. Can we afford not to take the risk of at least offering? Can we challenge our achievement-oriented, solution-focused culture and invest in looking at what's going on beneath the surface of so much, and such varied distress that manifests in ill-health, criminal behaviour and terrorist activities?

The first phone call, or email, from an enquiring client, turns the ignition.

At the moment contact is made work begins, even before agreeing a contract. From then on, how both parties respond to each other becomes the working relationship, the effectiveness of which depends upon care to all components.

The work is the same as the responsible therapist will be committed to herself, for her own sake and to protect clients from unknown, needy parts of her acting out in the relationship: for example, seeking approval in the form of positive feedback or seeking identity reassurance in the form of sexual contact (see Appendix, *Sex in the Forbidden Zone*).

Simply, the better I know myself the more substantial I feel, and the more fully I connect with others. This knowing includes the darker parts of my nature: the more I welcome my 'shadow' feelings (blame, jealousy, revenge), the less power these wield as a separate force and the less I need to box myself and others into being 'goodies' or 'baddies'.

CHAPTER TWO

STRUGGLE & SUFFERING

As I examined each working part of therapy, a question persisted. Could there be a common factor that brings each client to the therapy room?

What if all human distress, disturbance, discomfort and suffering emanated from one source, along infinitely various routes? If there was such a source, and we knew of it, could this knowledge benefit anyone and if so, how? Might I, as therapist, be tempted to work after all, towards eliminating this source if indeed it existed, rather than let it inform me? Might deeper knowledge of the human condition – of which suffering and pain, dying and death, are as valid parts of existence as joy and pleasure – help me relate more fully with myself and others? There are certainly dangers in generalisations. Yet if there is more to learn about our species, perhaps awareness itself would promote communication, globally as well as with one another as individuals.

In 2009, to mark the 150th anniversary of Darwin's 'On the Origin of Species', a torrent of information confirmed that all life-forms need certain conditions to survive. Like many creatures, humans depend upon members of the herd as well as on individual selves for food and shelter. Humans live in local tribes, have particular jobs within these to serve both selves and pack, and together with other tribes promote prosperity of the species. Inter-dependence, developing from extreme dependence in babyhood, continues throughout our lives, and extends far beyond human-to-human connection. In both the language of science that talks about sociability in terms of survival of the species, natural selection and the food chain, and of psychology that refers to emotional attachment (see Appendix, *Why Love Matters*), evidence is all around of mutual need and dependence, and of what happens when this need isn't fulfilled.

Humans seek out relationships and form attachments in a myriad of directions, create families and friendships and weave these contacts into the satisfaction of fundamental needs for food, shelter and protection. Indeed, dependence upon each other is an integral part of meeting all survival needs, including who we are on the most basic level, a sense of being a particular species. Our special identity. (There have been studies made of children reared by animals and their subsequent identity confusion.) Usually, from babyhood onwards, we form a sense of who we are, both similarities and personal differences, from being in relationship with others of our own kind.

As industrialised and computerised cultures have grown further and further away from living according to the natural law of inter-dependence that balances togetherness and individuality, we've come to live with increasing momentum according to the unnatural law of independence and self-reliance, from as young an age as possible. Two world wars, preceded and followed by more localised but equally horrific conflicts, have left entire generations mistrusting their fellow humans.

Add to this the peculiarly British stiff-upper-lip strategy of survival which was spread globally in the days of Empire (the 'no cry' rule continues to be fostered in its remnant of boarding-school tradition), and an innate suspicion of all that is

foreign and therefore unknown, the promotion of 'a-depend-
ence' and pride in managing alone has appeared in reaction to
be the obvious solution.

Mainstream child-rearing books continue to support this
method, however well-disguised in child-centred terminology,
advising parents to train even tiny babies to be independent,
that's to say less demanding, less needy; instruction manuals
about feeding and bed-time regimes have all but replaced our
instinctive nature that knows the different timbre to each cry. I
remember well my own fight against nature, refusing to let my
distraught self, breasts spilling milk, pick up my distraught baby
before finally 'giving in'. I was wired to keep a distance. Promot-
ing schooling from an increasingly young age also chivvies
children ahead of their natural development.

Relearning to trust instinct has to be fought for; the idea that
human reason knows best, that it makes us somehow superior
creatures, has taken a firm hold.

If relationship with others wasn't part of our survival drive,
why, when we're deprived of contact, or deprive ourselves out
of fear of the risks that intimacy carries, would we seek ways to
compensate. From self-soothing in the form of thumb-sucking,
nail-biting, cigarette-smoking and comfort-eating to seeking relationship through imaginary friends, spending hours on Face-
book or by drawing a face on a football, we persist in filling the
void. Solitary confinement is the most extreme torture, deliber-
ately used to force dependency and attachment on the very
people who incite terror and inflict pain (Stockholm syndrome).
Such is the need for contact, some can stay in an abusive relationship for years; or self-inflict pain to alter or distract from an
unbearable state of disconnection. Anything to reduce the most
debilitating dread of being utterly cut off and therefore exposed

and undefended.

The despair of being deprived of touch and helpless to self-soothe adequately is seen in the inert bodies and forlorn faces of orphaned babies abandoned in their cots; eventually they lose the momentum even to suck a thumb or rock, and wither away just as a plant dies without vital nutrients.

Yet – it is this very need for attachment to and dependence upon others that carries the greatest risk of disappointment, of betrayal, of experiencing primeval terror of abandonment and helplessness. When out of balance and frozen in conflict, the dual needs for trusting connection and self-reliance can potentially generate the very greatest suffering and lead to infinitely creative ways of trying to escape this state that actually perpetuate it. Negotiating for balance is a way of living that I call *Autonomous Dependence* which begins at birth and continues up to and including our last heartbeat, breath and synaptic impulse.

If imbalance of these needs is, as I believe, the core source of suffering, for as long as we collude to ignore our cries for collaborative connection and continue to fight each other to the death for individual ownership, symptoms will become increasingly problematic. Too much of one and too little of the other at any given moment, whichever way the imbalance, we feel disturbed, bewildered and lost. We have a choice: to escape these feelings by any means we can devise or use them as information. Individually, the place of balance differs, and differs moment by moment. It is not static. As a pack, the place of balance varies too, and may not correspond with individual needs, or those of other packs. Hence inevitable conflict, just as every family knows.

What we can do is listen, learn to recognise imbalance,

contain automatic aggressive reaction and respond from body and mind together – and commit to this practice.

Is there a more devastating experience than let down (of fundamental expectations) by whatever or whoever we trust in, especially by our own kind? The deeper the trust and the closer the relationship, the greater the let down? The less the forewarning, the greater the shock? If there are physical wounds, and these heal, still how can we trust anybody at all, even or especially a close friend, never mind he or she isn't the person or institution we were injured by? Wouldn't we be stupid to? Isn't it wiser by far to depend on no one, keep friendships light and avoid intimacy? How, even if we want to get involved, can we trust ourselves to know better next time? Might instinct let us down? Do we want to take the risk of being devastated all over again?

Betrayal is a strong word. Yet betrayed – hurt, abandoned and helpless – is, to a greater or lesser extent, what I feel if a well-trodden neural pathway in the brain is hit by an unexpected experience: every year, the sun has shone on holiday; this year, it pours with rain. I can take it personally, feel betrayed by the weather, blame the weather-forecasters and then blame myself for being stupid. (I chose this example to show how a past, life-threatening betrayal can cross over to a closely-related pathway of disappointment that is harm-free.)

Blame and rage, directed outward at who or whatever is available and inward at the self, pour in to reinflate the hole left by shock; anything to recover a sense of power. Anything rather than remain caved in feeling helpless – unless this can somehow serve survival. In scientific terms, the sympathetic nervous system, having registered jolt to or severance of a pathway, pumps out survival-serving chemicals that circulate in the system shouting 'do something'.

The two central drives for belonging and for autonomy that when in balance promote optimum safety, therefore carry potentially torturing conflict between longing for and dread of being looked after, *and* between longing for and terror of independence. I propose these double conflicts to be the core common denominator which consciously or unconsciously motivates someone to seek out a therapist to discover whether, and if so how, he can reconcile and rebalance both survival drives in a way that allows for trust in and tolerance of natural pain and sorrow inherent to being alive; and make room for trust in and tolerance of joy. More used to leaping to solutions than enduring conflict, we tend to settle either for a life of closed-off independence or be sucked in to parasitic relationships; or to swing between clinging to and spurning contact. Extreme polarities are the hallmark symptom of borderline-personality diagnosis, and in terms of manic and depressive phases of its close cousin, the bi-polar pendulum.

Could it be, then, that whatever a new client declares as problematic is his particular way of introducing this conflict? That the unique individual details of his story show both drives clamouring for recognition? Restoring trust, in others and self, is arguably the essence of therapeutic work that facilitates Autonomous Dependence: relearning to trust our own instinctive nature and that of the pack, sniffing out danger when it's really there, responding accordingly and relaxing when it isn't.

Innately inquisitive creatures about the wider world, humans ask, 'What is the universe made of?' 'How did it start?' 'How does a bird fly?' 'How does an engine work?' All these questions require looking inside, breaking down, taking apart. Our own creature-nature invites and tolerates investigation as a species; it shies away from one-to-one inspection. Sneering at others for 'navel-gazing' and criticising 'self-indulgence' are fierce defences against being rendered exposed and vulnerable.

Mistrusting ourselves and others in the wake of so much betrayal on a global scale, independence and happiness have become the 'holy grail'. No wonder this way of surviving has been attributed to a 'selfish gene'. But calls of distress from our selves and our environment persist. The question, then, is how to answer in ways that make individual attention more tolerable, more personal and more joined up to the bigger picture. The more that disciplines and practices such as neuroscience and philosophy, psychiatry and psychotherapy can work towards collaborating rather than fighting each other to 'know best', towards allowing for and benefiting from difference and pooling resources, the greater the benefit to ourselves and our planet.

PART TWO

Demonstration

*the identifying characteristics of all
concerned have been changed*

CHAPTER THREE

MEETING & THE EARLY STAGES

My relationship with Sam began the moment he answered my phone call to book an appointment. In the week between speaking and meeting in person, I became increasingly nervous. All I had to go on was his voice, a deep base with a hint of accent I couldn't place.

June 1998: I woke up early, stomach thumping. Rather than hang around at home drinking coffee and worrying about road-works and traffic jams, I set off long before I'd planned. Since there were no hold-ups and even less traffic than usual, I turned into the bumpy drive of the therapy centre with a full hour to wait here instead.

It was eight o'clock, there were no other cars in the courtyard. I parked under an oak tree and peered around. Sam's directions had been good but still I hadn't expected such a rural location.

Now what? What if someone saw my car and came to question what I was doing so early? I got out and strode back up the track trying to look purposeful even though I felt like a trespasser. Up and down I went, checking to see if I was being watched. I returned to my car with relief and got busy with the contents of my handbag. My diary could usually occupy ten minutes or so. At a quarter to nine, another car drove in, an ancient grey Peugeot. This had to be him. My heart bumped a little harder. In my rear-view mirror, I watched a tall man lope across the cobbles. Hmm, nice denim jacket and no briefcase, just a folder under one arm and a thermos in his other hand. He stopped at the nearest barn door, heaved it open and stepped inside. I took note that it hadn't been locked.

At one minute to nine, I knocked.

'Come on in.' Yes, I recognised the voice. Nice.

I stepped from bright sunlight into a dimly-lit room and stood still, heart now pounding. I had two things to hide: being posh, a source of shame all my life, and something I hadn't expected, an instant crush that I didn't want to admit to myself, let alone show. What was it about swarthy men with moustaches?

'Do you want to sit on cushions or do you prefer chairs?'

Sam was standing, shoes discarded, in front of a low rickety-looking table.

Some choice. I wasn't ready to sit at all. Not wanting to betray my accent, I didn't answer. I stood, sniffing at the musty smell of damp carpet and stale joss sticks, noting dead flies on the window-sill, a rusty electric fire in one corner and a pile of dingy mattresses and cushions. Therapy, rural Somerset, I knew the rules; I dragged a faded cushion to the middle of the room and plonked myself down. Sam sank down opposite and sat cross-legged. A quick glimpse at pale grey eyes and I lowered mine. Now I was faced with his open crotch two feet away. I shifted my gaze from black jeans to carpet.

'I suppose it all goes back to when I was five,' I muttered to the floor, picking at the drab matting. I had to start somewhere. I didn't really know what I was here for. Guilt, mostly, that I was more than halfway through my counselling training and all I seemed to do was weep in front of my fellow-students.

From the outside, my life would indeed be called privileged:

married and supported, plenty to eat, comfortable house, healthy children; my childhood too: private education, boarding schools, parents who were divorced, yes, but not dead and who still spoke to each other, no shouting. But something was missing. This was the only way I could describe underlying dissatisfaction I daren't complain about for fear of being called spoilt, both by family and friends and by myself.

It wasn't so much that I was searching for meaning in my life; I just wanted to feel involved and be part of something, rather than sit on the outside staring in at other people with envy, their jobs even more than how they looked.

Crunched up on my cushion, I recited a few details of family history: moving four times in my first five years, my father leaving, moving house and schools, moving again, and again, then off to prep school, public school and university; I mentioned my stepfather as an afterthought. I peeped up occasionally to check Sam's face. I dreaded laughter and a smile would be almost as bad. What I saw in the eyes opposite mine was interest; not the inquisitive kind that demanded information, but the patient kind that was waiting to see what came next.

'Why rake everything up now?' a familiar voice sighed into my right ear. I looked up at the clock. Five minutes left. I didn't want to go. There was something I liked about being here, despite the chill, the damp, and having nothing to lean against.

Then Sam said something I hadn't expected.

'It'll take more than a couple of sessions to do this work.'

I breathed out for what seemed like the first time that morning. I was being taken seriously. I still didn't want to leave but at least I could come back, as many times as I wanted. I'd pay somehow, raid the housekeeping, ask my mother.

'Same time next week?' Sam reached for his diary.

I nodded and slipped on my flip-flops, glancing again at the clock. One minute to ten. I scuttled out so I didn't have to be told to go.

* * *

That first taste of attention, a whole hour all for me, was like a grain of sugar given to a starving man. Over the first summer, my craving was unleashed. First came my request for more time. An hour became an hour and a half. By the autumn, I was going twice a week. And starting to lie, even when questioned about the mileage clock in my car. Each visit, I left home earlier than necessary, scared something would prevent me from arriving, not believing I'd really get there until I was safely parked under the oak tree. I knocked on the barn door as many minutes early as I hoped I could get away with.

To my five year-old self, Sam became my third-time-lucky dad. Since visits were inevitably regulated by the time he had and the money I could get hold of, I turned to cramming enough care-ration into each session to last the days in between.

In terms of addiction, frantic to fill the void inside, attention became my 'fix' rather than food or alcohol, frenetic activity or gambling. I was met by a therapist who set boundaries for himself so I could, by trial and error, find my own. I had to learn for myself what would and wouldn't fill this hole.

* * *

'Whatever are you writing?' I was asked at home each evening. I sensed a mixture of curiosity, bemusement and occasional impatience at my sudden and frenetic new activity.

'Nothing, just some notes,' I replied from the far end of the kitchen table, shielding my pages like a schoolgirl as I continued to scribble down long-forgotten memories I'd never before considered relevant. I was afraid of missing a single thought in case it slipped away again like an elusive dream. And keeping a diary wasn't enough; I turned to transcribing my notes into letters, my need to tell unstoppable.

Day after day, I posted bulging envelopes to the barn, hoping they'd reach Sam somehow, beginning to compose the next letter as soon as I walked away from the post box. I accused myself of cheating: I wasn't paying for his extra time. I accused myself of cowardice: I was writing things I daren't say aloud. And I didn't stop.

'I'm sorry,' he said when I arrived one Monday after a particularly detailed confession; everything I divulged felt that way. I looked up from the carpet. This was a sorry I could hear, not the pitying kind but simply minding. For a second, I felt just a little bit special. I liked that.

October 1998: 'You're going to be my father, brother, lover, friend,' I declared from my cushion.

'I wish all my clients knew that,' Sam replied.

I swelled with pride. Then swerved to another thought: hmm, other clients? I didn't like that, I wanted to be the one-and-only. Or if not, certainly be the most important.

November 1998: 'I know I'm going to try and seduce you,' I announced looking directly into Sam's eyes, back straight, hoping he'd appreciate my honesty. I knew myself well from student days. This had always worked, to feel wanted, to get cuddled, to feel not just special but proud of myself. Even if I'd found kissing revolting and sex plain weird.

'Then let's make a deal, that we don't have sex,' Sam answered, holding out his hand. I took it; we shook and smiled at each other. Now it remained to be seen whether he'd stick to this deal, however hard I tried to make him break it.

* * *

Our relationship became a testing-ground. I spent the drive and my hour's wait in the car park juddering with fear that he would forget the time or be late or somehow our session would be stolen. The closer to starting time, the fiercer my pumping heart. Sometimes I walked to the corner of the lane to watch for him. Occasionally I hitched a ride in his Peugeot down the bumpy drive to grab a couple of extra minutes and to gain further access into his life. However many times Sam proved himself reliable, my dread of missing out didn't abate.

Without realising this was what I was doing, I was instinctively creating situations similar enough to activate feelings, different enough to have a chance of learning something new. Hence, arriving early to wait for my 'dad'. Hence, flirting with my 'step-dad'.

* * *

'I know I'm pushing for a 'No',' I told Sam one morning, aware that sharing my secret might bring the dreaded 'no' that much closer, but needing him to know it.

My hunger for attention was being fed. Now I wanted touch; I wanted to be cuddled. ('Never satisfied,' moaned the voice that sat on my right shoulder, alternately exasperated or critical, terrified of what I might drag up or do next.) Shame prevented me from asking Sam outright. Would he want to? He might be disgusted at the idea. Might he refuse by hiding behind some therapy-rule? He might think this was me trying to seduce him and laugh. ('Well, isn't it? You don't fool me.')

I introduced the subject by way of recounting a recent dream in which Sam and I were sitting in the back of a car holding hands in a friendly, comforting way; the woman in the front, raven-haired with scarlet lips and nails, turned round to smirk, full of sexual innuendo. I named her The Vamp. I knew her well.

My need exposed, I curled up tight, in that moment too sensitive for any touch at all. Luckily, Sam didn't, he talked instead. I didn't understand much of what he said about 'split-off sensuality' and 'sexualising all contact', but as I drove home some of his words began to make sense. No wonder I'd always dreaded being told sexy jokes, felt embarrassed if I'd understood and stupid if I hadn't, pretended to laugh, afraid of naivety being exposed.

I still didn't ask directly for a cuddle, despite yearning. Week by week, I kept on hinting. When I arrived, I dragged mattresses together, piled up cushions and made a nest for us both to sit in. I was getting closer.

'It's like coming home, walking in here,' I mumbled as I built our house. Each week, I'd been bringing things to make my mark: a vase, then flowers to put in it; shells to line the window-sill, just a few, careful to pace my encroaching presence so I wouldn't be turned out. In the same way, I gauged my requests to what I thought Sam would concede to. The fleeting idea he could be enjoying my company brought another set of fears; almost better to be a nuisance.

'Every time you come, you bring something with you,' Sam remarked one morning. I flinched. Didn't he want my gifts? It was how I showed affection. Leaving things behind was how I made sure he wouldn't forget me. Carrying things as I entered helped me feel less naked. At least he didn't tell me to stop, so I didn't.

Christmas was coming. How would I survive with no contact at all for two whole weeks? Four days was hard enough to endure pining for the musty barn. I wanted a photograph. I wanted to tape sessions. Each request was agony to squeeze out.

'I hate being so needy,' I wailed.

'We must take care of the needy little girl in any way that's ethical,' Sam replied.

I survived the break by colouring in an hour chart like the ones I'd made towards the end of term at school and by replaying his voice on my ancient tape-recorder.

'Do you think I'm going to die?' Sam's voice crackled through my headphones. Morning after morning, hours before dawn broke I slunk downstairs to sit by the Rayburn, cat on my knee, my family safely asleep.

'No, it's not that.' What a stupid idea. 'I just... I did bring my camera. Of course, I could manage without a picture.'

'Let's go take a photograph,' rumbled Sam's voice, followed by scuffles, the door slamming, a moment's silence during which I pictured slipping into the courtyard; Sam had stood with his arms folded in front of the barn door – the picture was now on my lap – while I had glanced furtively round to see if anyone was watching me press the shutter before scurrying back inside. I could sense The Vamp smirking. I listened to my panting voice say 'Thank you,' and Sam's reply, 'You're welcome. And, I'll see you in two weeks.' I rewound the tape, sipped my tea, and watched the sky lighten through the kitchen window.

It didn't matter there wasn't regular post or that Sam was on holiday; I continued writing letters, one, often two each day. On top of which, as if my hand had grown a life of its own, I began to scribble down rhymes. Not poems. More like nursery-rhymes.

* * *

The child within me was responding to Sam's attention with increasing hunger for closeness, not only in terms of cuddles but by remembering the unknowable in whatever form possible to share. Memories surfaced not as clear events in tidy order, but in dreams and images. This, it seems, is how repressed and forgotten experiences are retrieved from the more primitive parts of the brain that respond to and hence encode trauma (see Appendix, The Emotional Brain).

Despite ignoring Sam's reference to dying, the expression 'missing, presumed dead' began to fit my father's disappearance for the six months between leaving and turning up for Christmas. I was terrified that Sam would disappear, never to return. I had to stop that ever happening again.

My nightmares were like horror movies, of being stalked and grabbed; all that was missing was creepy music. I awoke in cold sweats, fighting to move my legs as I emerged into wakefulness.

The one I brought not only to therapy but also to my training group when I had the chance was as follows: 'I am in a crowd of people, trying to see what's happening. I fight to the front and see a boy, aged about nine, lying staked out in a trough. He's in his underpants, I notice his penis is not erect. There's hot liquid seeping towards one side of him, he strains to escape it but cannot. He strains to make noise but his lips are squeezed shut. And I cannot rescue him.'

The choice of rhymes as another medium, I attribute to a part of me I started calling The Wise One. She came up with a way of keeping the content contained, the sing-song rhythms (I'd grown up with Hoffmann's Strewwelpeter on my bookshelf) making the unspeakable at least writable, to be shown if not read aloud to Sam.

* * *

January 1999: Huddled on a mattress, shrouded in blankets, I read the first line of one rhyme aloud and stopped halfway along the second. That was plenty. 'Thump, thump, the ogre comes, Smacking his lips…'

'Just let them out, write them down and show me,' Sam encouraged. So I did. Page after page, week after week they poured out. I brought them with me and left them with Sam for safe keeping. I didn't know, and didn't ask, if he read them all through; or my letters either.

'What's the liquid?' asked Sam when I read out my nightmare.

The answer wouldn't squeeze through clamped jaw.

'That's semen on the bed,' he said. I kept still, breath shallow. I had no speakable language for sexual body parts, let alone functions. I nodded.

The following session, I drew a picture of me staked out and labelled it like a biology diagram. We stuck it to the inside of Sam's cupboard door. In the next training session, safe amongst tutors and peers, I acted the dream. The colleague I was working with invited me to get up and push against him, so I pushed and pushed until I was spent. In silence, lips clenched.

My need to be cuddled by Sam just had to be spoken. I hinted more directly.

'I want...' I crept a bit closer. I tried again. 'I feel lonely over here. I wish...' Silence. Breathing. Please understand.

'Of course, how stupid of me. You want to be held,' said Sam. He reached forward. At last he'd got the message.

Scooped up with his arms wrapped around me I whispered, 'I want to be as inside as possible.'

And so I was. Cocooned. This was where I felt safe enough to tell him what I'd needed protecting from.

February 1999: 'Everybody goes,' I mumbled to the mattress cover. ('Nonsense.' The voice on my shoulder was severe today.)

'Tell me who?' Sam murmured.

I leapt up and rushed across to the wall, scrabbling at the cold stone with my fingernails. Time to shout.

'My nanny, my father, my stepfather... my mother.' The last word spurted out as a shriek. I flung my arms around my head. Blasphemy.

* * *

Disintegration: *This was a pivotal moment. My truth being spoken and heard brought it alive, gave it reality. Connection to the person I'd lived as for forty years was severed. I was left with no link other than my name was still Jane (which I didn't like since it had a severe ring left over from schooldays). Stripping myself of myths that had served to protect me all my life, my need to attach and cling somewhere rendered me at Sam's mercy. And cling I did. Literally, physically, like a limpet.*

What an opportunity for Sam to play with my need (as my stepfather had done), to use it to fill some personal void (as an unaware or power-seeking therapist might do). Someone terrified by such extreme anguish might have suggested medication. Sam simply let me cling, for as long as it took for me to reconstruct my sense of who I was.

It's this part of the process, being dependent, that uncertain therapists often criticise and the general public mistrusts. The value of experiencing the fear of intense emotional need and being met (attended to, not given in to) rather than abused or shunned, cannot be matched. If dependence has ever been experienced as unsafe, to feel dependent safely is an integral part of the unlearning-relearning process vital for reinstating survival mechanisms.

* * *

'How can I become independent without being dependent first?' As scary as being this needy was, I determined to live what seemed so obvious.

Sam nodded.

Good.

* * *

At the time, this transition seemed entirely linear. Of course, I was seeing with child-eyes. Nevertheless, my understanding of the process of growing up came, I believe, from a universal wisdom stitched into our genetic make-up. That Sam could be with me through this clingy stage was a gift I'm sure came both from his own ability to maintain boundaries, with support as and when needed (I questioned him about supervision), so we weren't consumed by my ravenous hunger; and from his trust that I wouldn't remain stuck here. I'd only cling 'forever' if I was pushed away; allowed to cling and my natural impulse to widen my focus would emerge. Nevertheless, it was risky. Some factor beyond either of us could have interrupted this process. In which case, would I have found somewhere else to cling?

I had little sense of my adult self in these months though hard-wired functioning didn't let me down: I continued to drive competently as well as shop and cook even though I did as little as I could get away with to allow for writing.

* * *

'I need more adult,' Sam said as I sulked the whole way through a session.

'She's not here.' I stamped my foot. Talking with a woman the other side of the courtyard – I'd been in my car watching through the rear-view mirror – had made Sam two minutes late. His apology had made no difference.

I left, precisely on time as usual, forgoing my goodbye hug.

* * *

As I fought to make up for the cuddles I had missed and longed for as a little girl (in terms of gambling addiction, I was chasing losses), I subjected myself to another dose of abandonment, by myself this time. This came in the form of hating.

As instantly as if I'd waved a magic wand, Sam had become the centre of my universe and my hero. Would he survive my hate?

'Lovely Mummy, horrid Daddy… lovely Daddy, horrid Mummy,' I

had chanted as a seven year-old, whirling between sofas in the drawing room as my father sipped tea after an outing, about to leave.

So I ricocheted between loving and hating Sam. Could I come to bear knowing him as less-than-perfect without relegating him permanently to the hate-bin? Could I take on some responsibility for my own care and discover that wouldn't make him care any less?

Perhaps this would depend on how he coped with my jealousy.

* * *

'I want it all for me,' I wailed. ('Greedy-guts,' hissed the voice down my ear.) How dare Sam give the client before me an extra five minutes. I'd been parked and waiting-and-watching as usual. At least it had been a man emerging through the barn door, not a sexy, irresistible blonde. But a man wasn't much better.

'It was my time,' I screamed the moment I was through the door. 'Well,' I backtracked, fearing I'd miss yet another cuddle, 'I know it wasn't really...'

'No, keep going.'

I couldn't say any more to Sam's face. I turned my back and spoke as if we were on the telephone. 'Fuck you,' I yelled, then flung myself onto a cushion in the corner of the room, arms shielding my head against inevitable beating. What came, instead, was a soothing murmur.

'You certainly crossed an edge there.'

'I want... to be special,' I wailed on. 'No, I want to be the special-*est*.' That was it. Didn't that mean having to annihilate all rivals? How else could I be the one?

March 1999: 'I want... I know you're not my father and I know I'm not...' Could Sam fill in the dots?

'You want me to love you, don't you? Well, I do... but I'm afraid it won't be enough.'

55

Of course it would.

'Don't say it if you don't mean it, you can take it back…'

'Oh, Janey,' he sighed.

Well, what did I know? People seemed to do that all the time. Didn't they?

Anyway, I'd got what I wanted and it was plenty.

Sam loving me did last but… it didn't fill the 'something's missing' place. So, he loved me. Perhaps he loved other clients too. In which case, my ration wasn't nearly enough. 'If I can't have it all, I don't want any,' I scribbled in my book of rhymes.

* * *

Straining for the non-existent status of one-and-only was how I kept Sam distant, how I kept myself safe by not letting his love stick. Each hint I got that other clients existed, even worse, that he had relationships outside work and worst of all that he was married, I hurtled down a tube of jealousy, hating my rivals and hating Sam for having a life (even for taking a sip of water). Hate was very effective in keeping Sam out of my heart. The cell I condemned myself to protected me; if I couldn't physically stop him leaving, I could refuse to mind if he did.

I would continue to use this strategy until I realised not only that I could survive but already had survived my caretakers' absence.

* * *

Having pushed Sam away, I turned to one of my tutors for comfort (the man, not the woman). Safe. Huggy. No shameful crush to manage.

'When you start letting your therapist's care in, you won't keep on needing more,' he said.

* * *

This goes for all addictions, all objects of desire, all illusions that to obtain will fill and fix (loss of and need for contact and safety). To open to Sam's care meant – hence fierce resistance – realising and feeling (accepting) the loss of what had once been missing. No wonder the tor-turing conflict between clinging and pushing away; no wonder the wish to not-need when needing felt so risky and the attempts to control Sam's comings and goings when my emotions were governed by all he did and said (see Appendix, Trauma and Recovery). Many times I heard Sam say, 'I won't stop'. And he didn't. However hard I fended off, so long as I kept coming his care would seep through. So I did.

* * *

June 1999: I spied a teddy bear in the corner of the room. Yes, it was Sam's. Yes, the client before me had held it. Huh. In that case, I wanted to take it home with me.

I hinted in my well-practised way that avoided the shame of being turned down. Noticing she – yes, a she-bear – had no eyes, I offered to make some.

'I can't let you take my bear home,' Sam said. I flushed. How dared he guess, and guess right. But this was too important to hate for long. There must be a way of having something that other client hadn't got.

'I could bring my sewing things in?'

'Ok, that's good, let's see what we can do.'

I drove home wondering whether I had made Sam give in. Or perhaps he hadn't given in at all; perhaps everything I asked for felt manipulative because that's what I was doing, manoeuvring around obstacles to get what I wanted rather than straight asking. I shuddered at the memory of being told to 'go and make love' to my stepfather, of his smirk as he lapped up the innuendo.

Perhaps Sam was simply giving, not giving in, because he

wanted to; and to encourage me to ask for what I wanted more directly.

For the three weeks it took to complete the operation on his bear, Sam and I played doctors and nurses each session, sitting close, engrossed in our task. I relaxed my guard.

* * *

Some months later, when I asked outright, Ted did come home for a visit! I got what I'd wanted, by different means. And it wasn't just me; Sam had come to trust (he told me) that I'd take care of something precious of his. Hey, I felt special. And I hadn't had to murder his other clients.

* * *

Summer-Autumn 1999: The child in me was feeling more secure with Sam but at home had become increasingly isolated.

Ignoring his early-on warning to be careful, I had revealed some of what I'd been writing about. Questions, concern, suggestions (to check Sam out, to seek medical opinions), more concern when I resisted – I heard it all as measures to prevent me having what had become as fundamental as air and water. I was adamant: I was going to continue this work and continue seeing the therapist I had chosen.

I pleaded for understanding. I yelled insults across the kitchen table. I took a deep breath and attempted to explain and précis the chaotic process of joining up resurfacing body sensations and emotions to long-ago memories. In between, I retreated to write, listen to tapes of sessions and count the days until my next one. Cooking and cleaning could wait.

As positions became more polarised and entrenched, mistrust turned to fear. I overheard hushed telephone conversations about what to do for the best and pictured men in white coats coming to get me.

Frantic, I wailed that there was nothing the matter with me: I was angry because no-one was listening; I cried, a lot, because I was lonely. 'I, I… what about everyone else?'

Huddling in the room I'd made my burrow, an idea began to take shape and it brought relief. No more trying to be who I was no longer.

* * *

Separating is, sometimes, where disclosure leads (and why, sometimes, therapy or the therapist gets blamed): conflicting agendas to meet the core need for safety. The engine of a relationship, stripped down and exposed, can be found to have essential parts damaged beyond repair, missing altogether or simply not robust enough for going 'off-road'.

* * *

Winter 1999-2000: It was time. I prepared to move out. I was aware the choice I was making broke the strongest taboo and blessed one friend for saying, 'It must be bad, for you to leave all this.' A mother of two small boys, she wasn't just meaning a five bed-roomed house and acre of garden.

'What kind of mother leaves her children?' the voice on my shoulder snarled. I began to recognise the relentless judgement as a form of self-harm, guilt serving to protect from the deeper pain of this particular separation which I dared not feel until after I had gone.

Time with Sam was spent playing bears and designing a future. I no more wanted to fill these hours howling than as a child I'd wanted to spoil precious outings and holidays being homesick.

* * *

Nature's wisdom: in extreme situations, pain is delayed until action has been taken.

* * *

It was now that I turned to my father. For eighteen months I'd been forming my own truths, relying on my experiences in the therapy room to tell me what was and wasn't so. Time to check out who my dad was.

I arranged to pay a visit. Memories of stilted school outings filled my long drive to Suffolk and I arrived with stomach churning. I had a warm greeting, from my stepmother as well as father; the three of us exchanged pleasantries over coffee and then lunch. I was keeping my questions for the afternoon walk. 'Nothing to lose, all to gain,' I kept reminding myself.

After washing up, my father and I strolled through the village and out onto a track into the woods. I paused by a gateway.

'Daddy, I know it's a long time ago but I need to know, about you leaving… about us, me…'

'Janey…' his voice was strained. He shifted his walking-stick to the other hand and cleared his throat. 'I had so much to think about, I was fighting for my job.'

Not good enough. 'Did you think about me, did you miss me at all?' My voice squeaked out with the effort of not crying.

'Of course I did, you were my little girl.'

Better, but still defensive. 'Why didn't you come to see me?'

'But I did, that first Christmas.'

I didn't know that. 'I don't remember,' I whispered.

'You clung and wailed when I left; you did that every time I visited. It broke my heart; I had to peel your arms from around my neck. Yes, there were long gaps between outings; it wasn't the same in those days, people didn't know so much about these things.'

My father leaned on the gate and gazed across the valley. 'Isn't it a glorious day?'

'I'll look at the day when we've finished,' I snapped back.

'Janey, I'm too old.' His voice was sharp. 'I've put all this behind me,' he added with a sigh.

'Well, I haven't.' I was trembling. The final test. 'Maybe I'd better go.'

'Maybe you had.'

That wasn't right. I felt a trickle between my legs which were now trembling. One last fight.

'Please…,' I wailed. Silence. I looked down and held my breath.

My father held out his arm, 'Come on, let's walk on.'

I slipped my hand into the crook of his elbow, the closest contact for forty years. We walked slowly along the muddy track, shoulders touching, our voices calm now we were on the same side.

'I just need to know some things, then I can put it behind me too. Thank you.' But the rest could wait. On the way back, I paused at the same gate. 'Now I can look at the view. Yes, it's a lovely day.'

I had what I'd come for.

When I told Sam about our reunion, I checked carefully for signs of jealousy. It seemed, however, that I could have two parents after all – my Dad and my Sam. Another request began to form.

At home, I filled the spare room with boxes of books, discarded toys and photograph albums. Preparing to pack, I felt emptier and hungrier. I spied an empty photograph frame, searched for a piece of thick paper, found a stray felt-tip pen in the kitchen and began writing.

'I Jane…' I wrote using my left hand and drew lines of swirls and squiggles as if I was eight designing an ancient document for history class.

The second paragraph began 'I Sam…' and continued in the same way. I made two lines of dots for our signatures and cut the paper, rough like parchment, to fit the frame.

The following Monday, I placed the certificate on the floor between Sam and myself without speaking. This was how I broached our mutual adoption. I knew he wouldn't just sign, he'd talk about what I was asking for and if he wanted to, but that was alright. I'd rather a 'no' than pretending. I wanted him to be my dad for real, to feel-mean it. His declaration of love hadn't run out exactly, but I wanted commitment, the forever kind.

I left the document with him. Meanwhile, I came up with something else. I began writing stories about Fairytale Cottage, a magic place for just the two of us, father and daughter together. No visitors. No goodbyes. I conjured up each room, furnished and decorated them one by one; our days always ended with Sam reading aloud as I snuggled in bed, him in the chair at my side.

* * *

Creative therapy. Ideas from both parties, the client's the ones with the greatest opportunities for unlearning and relearning.

In therapeutic language, a transitional object is anything that helps maintain connection. Fairytale Cottage helped me through transition to a life of singledom. I needed some sense of stability so I didn't try to run back to where I'd once been safe but was no longer, and I found this in fantasy. However, this wasn't a lone fantasy; I shared it and Sam entered into my game fully, adding his own stories. Thus, we made it ours, though ever mindful of it having started as mine. Like giving his bear eyes. Something else valuable, too: by loving me and by sharing my fantasy in the woods Sam made himself vulnerable.

Joint investment and risk-taking, by therapist as well as client, lies at the heart of therapy.

* * *

May 30th 2000: I had arranged my moving date for half-term when the house would be empty and so I'd be gone when the family returned.

I woke to early drizzle. Slowly, I put the kettle on for the last time, cleaned my teeth and said goodbye to the basin, said goodbye to my bed in the spare room before closing the door. These were goodbyes I could bear.

Two removal vans trundled up the drive and suddenly there were men asking questions about different-coloured labels and emptying rooms. I felt greedy and guilty watching the vans being loaded. I talked myself round, remembering my lawyer saying I was allowed my share. There'd certainly be no going back for second helpings. I scurried through the house rearranging pictures, shifting remaining chairs and spreading ornaments out across the mantelpiece in a vain attempt to cover over and fill in the gaps.

It was the sight of a smelly trainer, discarded in the hall, which threatened to unblock the howl compressed just below my throat. It looked lonely. I turned away.

The vans were ready to leave. I had to lead the way. 'Give me a minute,' I called. I looked around the kitchen I could no longer call mine; my feet, without any conscious command from my brain walked slowly outside. I turned to lock the door and posted the key through the letter-box.

My friend's voice echoed again. Yes, it had been bad. Yes, I did need to go.

'It'll be alright,' I chanted to myself as I bumped over the potholes down the drive and all the way to my new home, seven miles away.

CHAPTER FOUR

THE MIDDLE YEARS

The first months alone, I was a child playing house. I enjoyed arranging my kitchen cupboards, dusting my ancient television and eating what and when I liked, none of which involved cooking. I was all cooked out. I painted each room and gradually replaced alien smells with my own. I imagined inviting Sam to tea. Then I did. He accepted.

* * *

As close as it was possible without crossing ethical boundaries, Fairytale Cottage did for a moment come true. As always, there was a difference between what I longed for (to turn the clock back) and what happened: Sam was not my fantasy-replacement dad who had come back for me. The point was, could I absorb the benefits of the present enough to cease chasing the past?

* * *

We sat on my second hand, new-to-me white sofa, sipping tea and eating home-made, not-by-me buns. An hour later, I stood at the sitting room window watching him walk to his car and drive away, my own arms restraining me from running out yelling, 'Don't go.'

* * *

The vacuum in me could not be filled, by him, or by any efforts of mine.

Sam had been right. All his love and care was not enough, on its own. He could not be full-time and exclusive mother-father to my little girl even after we'd both signed those adoption papers to honour this extra-special relationship. For I was neither just little nor was I helpless, however hard I wanted to be as the only way I knew to get looked after.

There was nothing more to add that would turn extra-special into special-est, that non-existent prize (which, if it did by magic materialise, would surely be the pinnacle in terms of isolation from one's species). Indeed, I was wondering whether there was a hierarchy of specialness at all. Perhaps my striving had been serving as distraction from the scarier task. Perhaps it was time to risk digesting Sam's love and care and allow myself to feel special. Of course, how simple.

The child in me fought against this idea, tooth and nail, literally.

* * *

Autumn 2000: The method I chose to distract and divert myself from longing – for my children, for my mother, for Sam – was clawing my skin. When no cuddles were available and my next session with Sam was days away, I went upstairs to my duck-egg blue bathroom and scraped my nails up my legs, across my stomach and down the sides of my face. Mesmerized, I watched dots of blood ooze through the skin and trickle in rivulets. I chose the locations carefully, for as much I longed for large doses of 'poor you', 'what's the matter' and 'there-there', I dared not let anyone see, my face especially; my fear of those men in white coats lingered.

Pressure temporarily reduced, capacity to think and reflect returned – about the essential need for safety; about the need for reliable adult presence to provide that safety and the terror when that presence isn't there; about child-dependence in adult-hood, my own especially. And how fear of the 'big wide world', or more exactly dread of making a fool of myself in it, had kept me home-bound, alternately relieved, guilty and frustrated.

Being little now I was living alone was not serving me well. At night, I lay trembling as windows rattled in the wind. Memories of Sam insisting 'I need some adult' was hitting home. I was missing me as well as missing my children.

* * *

Reconstruction: *From here on I began to form some shape. Since playing bears with Sam, and since crying out some of what seemed like a bottomless pond of tears (Alice comes to mind), I had gradually accumulated a whole family of my own; each bear represented a separate part of me that became more distinct as she emerged to be recognised, welcomed and named – one by one not at random, but in an order beyond my conscious selection.*

* * *

'Let me introduce you to Spike.' I pulled a small, scruffy-haired bear from my bag, dressed in a green velvet waistcoat, and plonked it on the mattress. My eight year-old tomboy sat with eyes gleaming, its frown challenging.

'Well, hello you. Good to meet you.' Sam did not pick Spike up, he knew to wait to be invited.

The following week the younger sister arrived. Molly was paler, less robust, softer and plumper. My four/five year-old self gazed round-eyed, silently sucking her thumb waiting for her turn for a cuddle. I placed her at Spike's side, half an inch behind.

Polly followed. I'd knitted this one myself and she turned out misshapen, not resembling the pattern much at all. As quiet as little Molly, fourteen year-old Polly felt all wrong, hating how she looked on the outside (no wonder she never got a Valentine's card) and how she felt on the inside.

More knitting. A month later, Gloria came in, head and limbs loosely attached to a round body, bright blue and decorated with buttons for earrings. Here was the eighteen year-old student who wanted to discuss and argue and wonder about things, and be taken seriously. She wanted and didn't want a boyfriend; she was feisty and independent yet still cuddle-hungry.

* * *

Each me I presented told, piece by piece, both of who I was (I often referred to 'real me'), and of the characteristics I'd developed to keep myself safe. My balance of Autonomous Dependence had definitely favoured the former.

Sam told me how much easier it was to relate to me now each one had been identified and named. I continued to jump between them without warning, but he was better able to keep track and therefore respond in an age-appropriate way; he related to my adult-self (whether or not I felt her presence), by telling me when he couldn't keep pace. This encouraged me to slow down; there wasn't much point if Sam wasn't with me.

* * *

Christmas 2000: 'Here's your present,' announced Spike, muscling in as usual to be spokesman. Out of my bag came a long thin parcel.

'Fishing-rod? Walking-stick?' Sam gave it a prod.

'Open it,' demanded Spike, impatient to see her daddy's face when he pulled out a foot-long tube of mars bars.

'Wow, that's a mighty lot of chocolate. Thank you, honey.'

I felt the endearment flow through my body like warmed syrup, permeating my entire nest of Russian-doll selves.

Sam produced a small package from behind a cushion. 'Your turn. Go slowly, now.'

I knew what I wanted. I knew Sam knew, I'd been talking

about it for weeks. Could this be it? I tore at a corner of the shiny paper. Dark-brown fluff peeked through. Yes, it was. I slowed down. This package was too precious to miss savouring the unwrapping.

'I can see the head,' all of me squealed. I peeked up and saw Sam's delight. 'It's just like on the movies,' Spike giggled.

A moment later, I cradled my little baby bear in my hands. The last to arrive. With Tiny, my family was complete.

* * *

Or was it? I took a photograph and realised one bear was missing; she was badly needed. I could borrow Sam's she-bear but one day she'd have to go back for good. It was time to make my growth into adulthood a more conscious endeavour and more permanent. The practical side of me was coming on fine: I was learning to pay bills, phone a plumber, even go out to work. But the nurturing part of my mother-self was inconsistent and her absence allowed space for my old habits of self-deprivation.

* * *

At work, the counter kept me safe; I enjoyed chatting, flirting even, with the customers, Spike and Molly playing shopkeepers. Even out on the shop-floor, Polly-me felt protected by the uniform. She'd been growing her hair; now she started experimenting with styles. Make-up could come later.

I was startled to realise how my privileged upbringing had taught me to mistrust anyone I hadn't been formally introduced to. Ironic, I thought, that introductions hadn't ensured safety, anyway.

I found a name for where I'd come from; I called this place *'Poshland'*. As I strode down the high street to work, generations' worth of prejudice dropped away. I didn't need it anymore.

Each Saturday, I proudly collected my brown envelope; I had

never felt so well-off. I fingered the notes and placed them in piles. I drew up columns in my account book. How long could I make my wages last? What if they ran out? Even though my figures showed there was enough for the following month, buying food turned into a courtroom argument ('faggots or steak, what does she deserve?') that could result in returning the contents of my basket to the shelves and going home with nothing.

Wanting to know more about my scrooginess, I bought a copy of A Christmas Carol. I read about Scrooge's boyhood and wept.

I told Sam about what I called my 'hot chocolate challenge'.

'Brilliant,' was his reward.

Once a week, I vowed to go into a café. Being generous came very slowly. My stomach contracted as I counted out the coins. 'Treat yourself' was the mantra of a new friend I'd made in my afternoon writing class. Occasionally, I settled for cheap and found I'd wasted money rather than saved any. I persevered, knowing this was the route to becoming more special to myself. I became more particular; I discovered that the best-tasting was what made it the best value, regardless of price.

One Sunday, I went to tea with an elderly friend of my father's. Ex-public-school, army officer, diplomat: he exuded a mixture of affluence and self-neglect.

'May I have another cup?' I asked.

'Yes, of course, help yourself.'

I reached for the box of teabags.

'No, use that one again,' he barked behind my shoulder.

I jumped. I didn't know him well enough to protest or tease, however gently. I returned home to write a piece on privilege and deprivation – by now I was writing a regular column for the journal Self & Society (see Appendix) – subtitled *Repetitive Teabag Syndrome.*

Being generous to others was an even stronger wrestle. I continued to live the lie which more of me believed than didn't, that I couldn't afford presents without going hungry or cold myself. I had, however, stopped giving myself a hard time for being mean; I'd be generous when I was ready and not before. That didn't mean waiting until I'd accumulated lots, but until I trusted a bit more that there was enough to go round, for me and for my friends. Giving because I 'was supposed to', if my heart wasn't in it, wouldn't work and just set me grumbling.

Sam's words from two years before returned as an echo: 'How can you relate to the wider world if you cannot relate to yourself.' In every area, it seemed.

Meanwhile, he continued to demonstrate generosity by giving far more than the time I was paying for. And I wrote another article called *Sacrifice.*

* * *

The neuroscientific findings which underpin my process of re-membering segmented parts concern shock. The startle reflex (most easily seen in new-born babies' flung-out limbs) activates the pumping up of chemicals needed to mobilise the Fight/Flight response, noise included. If no action is necessary, this arousal lowers by means of shaking, releasing the held breath, crying, sobbing – often eased by being gathered up and held in some way. Completion of trauma is a matter of reconnecting to our senses, to our tribe, to the environment, ultimately to entire existence.

Unless released, either from mobilising to fight or flee or by shaking out body-tension which is no longer required, the ready-for-action position (chemically quite different from that of relaxed alertness) is held: both body and mind remain in that poised state and in time that state becomes fixed and assumes a power of its own. The tension itself becomes separated (a form of 'forgetting') from its source and can last for as long as a life-time if unaddressed, sapping energy and producing a host of physical symptoms (unexplained back-ache, headache, depression, migraine, chronic-fatigue, to name a few) and destructive behaviours. These calls for attention to the back-story can fall on deaf ears; the drive to alleviate pain and distress can exclude what lies beyond. Living in a state of unneeded but unreleased tension becomes normalised; as it becomes easier to settle for what is than fight for what could be, the origins of discomfort slip from awareness, eclipsed by current symptoms.

As a culture, we're well-practised in soldiering on, not fussing and putting up with. There's a valid place for this (on the battlefield), but prolonged 'playing dead' when no longer necessary exacts further cost.

At the heart of an experience of unresolved trauma – whether this be a single catastrophic event or a continuing experience of entrapment – lies helplessness: if Fight or Flight in the face of danger is impossible, for whatever reason, sooner or later the Freeze response collapses into resignation (not to be confused with acceptance); the held breath must exhale, if only minimally enough to sustain life. This state of helplessness is one of despair, only survivable by developing ways of managing, including fighting other people's battles to compensate. Managing does draw out creative resourcefulness; there is also invariably loss as well as gain: for example, eking out rations (of food and cuddles) as if still in short supply kept me deprived, extending suffering. In effect, I'd become my own jailor. Realising this was my key; only I had the power to release myself.

Perceiving threat is experienced as real as physically-obvious danger and the chemical arousal and emotions are the same. Imagine a baby who screams at a feather or a child who freezes in face of a spider: imagine his fear being dismissed or mocked or reasoned away by an adult equally horrified, if not of the feather or spider, then by the scream that triggers his or her own baby-self panic.

Living with unreleased chemical arousal takes a lot of energy, including the means chosen to manage. All have some gain or pay-off; all carry a price in terms of vitality and interrelating.

'Survival personality' (see Appendix, The Making of Them) becomes entrenched unless or until enough soothing reduces the chemical flooding and the residue is mobilised.

It only takes one moment of extreme threat to unbalance severely trust in both environment and oneself in terms of safety. How, indeed whether, balance is restored depends upon the kind of attention and care available and accessed in the aftermath.

* * *

Christmas 2000 cont: I didn't want to manage the day alone. That year, for the first time since the Christmas I didn't remember, aged five and a half, I was with my father. He and I couldn't make up for what we'd both lost but we could enjoy each other now. What I'd been learning with Sam had been sinking in; time to try it out. The weekend was filled with magic. My father sensed me as more, a lot more, than the forty-five year-old woman who turned into his drive late after work on Christmas Eve.

'You may have even used this as a little girl,' he murmured, dangling an ancient knitted stocking. 'It was mine, Nanny made it.'

By the fire before breakfast the following morning, I unpacked something for each age of me: a fluffy rabbit, a sugar mouse, a puzzle, a pair of earrings, bath essence: something for everyone. Without me having had to ask, or explain.

Over the next two days, myth after myth melted away in front of the fireplace, reshaped and replaced by my own versions. What I'd wondered for a long time I became sure of: that each person's truth is true for them. Perhaps they didn't have to be exclusive. My next article would be called *Room for Both*.

Spring 2001: Another house-move, this time from Sam's barn. I was surprised I didn't become frantic, not even Molly. Over a couple of weeks, Sam and I packed up the treasures I'd brought there. Yes, I was sad to leave this musty, damp home, but not distraught. It wouldn't disappear.

For a few weeks, Sam and I camped in a temporary room. I was happier when we moved upstairs to the attic of the same building and settled in. The windows looked out at the sky, no one could look in. Spike and co. liked it immediately. I hauled up some extra cushions, refurnished the windowsill and found a corner to make home in. Only Polly-me trundled in without pleasure. It was her turn for attention.

'You don't know yet you're going to become a beautiful woman,' Sam said as I grumbled about how I looked, how I wanted to be like this friend, that person. 'Fourteen is a difficult age.'

Yeah, yeah, I'd heard that before. Curled over my hateful body (well, not completely hateful: I liked my hands and especially my feet, despite, or perhaps because of, being 'difficult'), I talked more about being a teenager first time around. Overweight, struggling to diet, I'd grown into my childhood nickname. Not that I was fat now, in fact my bum bones ground against the bottom of the bath, which Polly was extremely pleased about.

Out came the details of end-of-term weighing, a deliberate public humiliation for the fatties. I told of the time I'd starved for a week beforehand and was rewarded by losing half a stone; for once, I hadn't dreaded my games report being read.

Sam continued to insist I was just fine as I was, that changes would come naturally and I'd grow into myself.

When I finally dared take a peek in the mirror some months later, I was surprised. Not front-cover beautiful, but a glossy mane and something new about the eyes. If this was me, then I'd shed my frown mask. Time for a shopping trip.

Summer 2001: Taking care of myself was becoming less and less a chore. Almost surreptitiously as if this was self-betrayal, I occasionally took out a mixing bowl and beat together ingredients for cake. (I'd never stopped making bread. It didn't count as cooking. Pummelling dough was defiance: aged seventeen, refusing to be moulded into debutante material I'd played up in Madame's baking class, earning myself a week of washing dishes.) I made mess, cleared it up, took out warm buns and ate them. Slowly, tasting, swallowing, digesting – enjoying.

Heightened agitation gradually relaxed. Rarely now did Polly need to claw at her legs or face. This happened just once in Sam's presence.

'I cannot work with you if you do that,' he'd said.

I'd held my breath. Would he throw me out, after all? (Was that what I'd done it for, to get expelled? A means of escape?)

'It hurts me too much,' he'd added.

Relief had flooded in like the tide. Wow. He must really love me if he hurts when I hurt myself, I'd thought. The urge to scratch utterly gone, I'd sat quietly opposite this man who'd taken the risk of loving me. And since I now knew how much, to continue testing him in the way I just had would have amounted to abuse. Which he'd told me clearly he wouldn't tolerate. I'd recognised my fork in the road – go hunt for someone else to torment or take in Sam's message: loving you doesn't mean letting you hurt me.

Autumn 2001: Spike had more tests waiting in the wings, she wasn't finished yet. Ever since the very first session, she and her siblings had kept an eye on Sam's crotch. 'Crotch-gazing' (as well as being, I suspected, a universal and natural, albeit unspoken, curiosity) started in earnest from being asked by my stepfather to 'say if my flies are undone'. And being mesmerised by gaping pyjamas clutched together by nicotine-stained fingers.

What I wanted, and by now was able to tell Sam even this most secret of asks couched carefully enough to be askable, was for physical proof of his arousal *and* for him to do nothing. This and only this, I was sure, would tell me first that I was desirable, second that I wasn't at the mercy of his (or any man's) sexual urges, and third that if he was aroused it wasn't my job to satisfy him.

'Thing is, Jane, I don't have sexual feelings towards you.'

Sam's voice was gentle. It didn't stop me recoiling on my cushion and pulling my knees in to my chin. The opposite corner beckoned. It was Gloria who hesitated. A truth was tapping on the door of her mind and my forty-six year-old body was in agreement: I didn't feel desire for Sam either. To admit this aloud would be to lose sight of my objective, so I didn't. Besides, I assumed my admission would hurt his feelings, like mine had been.

I stayed put on my cushion, determined to struggle through this one instead of or before taking cover in my cage of hurt-'n-hate. I remembered Sam's long-ago speech about split-off sexuality. Minutes went by. My brain turned this way and that, certain there was a way through this jungle.

'The love we don't make, it is ours, isn't it?' I floundered, ready to cower at the first hint of mockery.

'Oh yes,' Sam breathed. 'Jane, you're a heart-breaker.'

That, with his tone of voice, would do. Whatever this was, it didn't belong to and couldn't be stolen by anyone else. Special.

* * *

Imagine if a therapist didn't realise his parental role here to acknowledge and encourage rather than shame and diminish budding sexuality, and hold boundaries. Imagine if he colluded with his client's belief that having sex was the way to heal. Can regulation prevent such abuse? Whatever rules or guidelines are put in place must reflect desire for safety in ways that don't inhibit opportunity for such vital, creative work.

* * *

Job done? Satisfied? The Vamp sneered at my pathetic attempts at seduction and succeeded in undermining even this extra-specialness. I had to come up with something stronger.

Spike took over. No one was going to have what she couldn't, even if she didn't want it. ('Dog in the manger'.) Jealousy of rival clients (siblings) had eased; their existence hadn't stolen anything from me after all. Jealousy of Sam's wife became centre-stage, eating me up image by image:

Spring 2002: 'Witch… bitch…' I screamed aloud from behind the steering wheel, waiting at traffic lights one Monday morning. Opposite me was Sam's wife's car; I recognised the number plate from the time he'd driven it to work.

In the driver's seat, alone, was a woman who had to be his wife. At that time of the morning, she had to be only minutes out of bed, a place out of bounds to me and where things happened I had no part in. This simply must not be; I couldn't, wouldn't, bear it.

I had enough adult presence to talk back to Spike as I sped along the motorway. 'It's ok, we'll go and tell him; now stop yelling or I'll run into something.'

Half an hour later I parked, glad I no longer needed to arrive more than fifteen minutes early. I endured the wait by pacing around the car park. I slammed into Sam's room on the dot of nine.

'Where do I go, what happens to me?' I wailed after I'd told him who I'd seen. 'When you've having sex,' I muttered in a shame-filled whisper.

Sam started to talk but I didn't hear much, I was busy preparing my case.

'When a baby's tiny, surely she needs all the attention, just for a while, so she can learn for herself how special she is. Doesn't that mean the adults putting their relationship on hold?' I meant sex.

'It's not about sacrifice.'

Sam's voice sounded…angry? No. Intense? Okay, I'd stay put and listen.

'When a baby's needs are met, she's content and comfortable and unaware of what her parents are doing. Her concern is all about herself and her own needs. Their pleasure in each other is not a loss to her; far from it, their love and intimacy are what she's grown from and then provide the environment she grows in.'

I growled. This 'no' was the hardest to date because all of me, even Spike though she wouldn't admit it, knew he was right. No one could have 'all' the attention without someone, generally the giver, going without. No wonder I'd loathed, and subsequently mocked, the concept of 'sharing nicely'. Sharing depended upon generosity, self-generosity, and trusting there was enough for all: enough heart. The story of loaves and fishes came to mind.

I started to ponder over my stepfather's behaviour in terms

of jealousy. I wondered, too, about the impact of his polarised moods (from huffing rage to slushy); and how Spike resembled, and differed from, the child inside the man I grew up with from the age of six.

Summer 2002: For months after Sam's clear 'no' I thought and wrote and retreated back to the safe place of no sex talk. Spike, meanwhile, gathered her gang together to devise another plan.

'Let's play weddings,' she said. This'd do it, surely.

And so we played. I called it our 'commitment ceremony'. Sam stayed with me, always curious, risking, trusting. We planned for weeks. We played proposals. We set a date. I hunted down a silky nightdress in a charity shop to wear as my gown; Sam brought in a smart shirt.

Autumn 2002: The big day came. I started changing out of my jeans and stopped. My body refused to follow the plan.

* * *

Sam had let me find my boundary. I'm as certain as I can be that if I hadn't found my own 'no' he would have. I'm glad to know that and glad I was the one to stop.

I believe my way of pushing for 'no' was right for me, risk included. My body remembered not only games I'd played but how they'd been sexualised; I'd given myself the chance to refuse.

CHAPTER FIVE

LEAVING

S **pring 2003:** In the aftermath of my latest re-enactment, I felt small and lost all over again. But this time I refused to be little at home on my own. I dialled the Samaritans and by the end of the first week my fingers could find the number without me looking. The response I received encouraged me to call without censor. And to make friends with a neighbour.

Weeks went by, hurting. I asked for, and was given, more from Sam: what had begun as a weekly phone call when I first moved house escalated into a nightly ritual of a message on my answerphone. One by one, he said goodnight to each of me by name. If I was home, which I usually was, I picked up and listened 'live' and whispered 'night-night' when he'd finished, before putting the receiver down.

Now and then, I told myself to give up this luxury. This was Spike, trying to ease the pain of Sam withdrawing after she'd got used to something nice, by withdrawing first.

'He won't just stop,' I reassured her. 'And we won't need this forever, I'll know when it's time to say 'that's enough, thank you'. The effect of these conversations, of which there were many and varied, helped me stay connected and by soothing, I felt soothed.

* * *

Generosity. Sacrifice. Even when Sam's calls incurred loss to himself (he told me once he'd given up a concert ticket), I believe his overall 'yes' to my request came from a 'yes, I want to do this' inside himself.

To hear 'no' inside and say 'yes' to someone isn't generous; a sacrifice not freely given demands payback, in guilt if nothing else. A hook. Sam was teaching me to listen to my body, to recognise what I wanted, and to have a choice of saying 'yes' to me even if it meant 'no' to someone else. All his 'yes's and 'no's I believe came from his internal questioning and listening, even the 'no's being gifts, of honesty and respect. The expression 'a no said with love' which had always puzzled me, took on meaning. I was getting the difference between fighting against someone else and fighting for myself.

* * *

I began to consider that perhaps, just maybe, Sam didn't love the child-me's any less for being little; perhaps he even loved these me's as they were. Maybe he didn't love me any less for having other people in his life, *even* his wife. Maybe, if I made more connections in my own life, I wouldn't feel so distraught when he was with someone else. Perhaps this was already happening. I had something else to check out, though.

'What if I meet someone and fall in love?'

I watched Sam ask himself, watched him take his time before looking up to answer me.

'Jane, two things will happen. I'll be very, very happy. And it'll break my heart.'

Wow. Big feelings.

June 2003: I relinquished our nightly goodnights. I knew I was ready when they had begun to feel superfluous: for example, if I'd been out playing tennis, stayed for a drink and chat and returned two hours after Sam had rung.

I took this as a sign of being ready to finish working with him altogether. What would I gain by staying?

July 2003: Perfect timing to test myself: could I really distinguish between being five and leaving Sam after five years? I told him I wanted to finish in September.

Speaking my intention out loud made it real. All of me heard and my body went into immediate and escalating panic: juddering stomach, tight throat and dread. As the prospect of saying goodbye drew closer, no amount of working out what was happening made a difference. Cognition had no impact on my internal scream, 'Don't make me go'.

It took me eight weeks to respond, overruled by the voice on my shoulder itching to say 'I told you so'. But weight loss was too drastic to ignore. If the prospect of leaving was this debilitating, something must be missing.

January 2004: I tried again. This time I gave six months notice. Perhaps this would make a difference.

However, I delayed setting a date for our last session and didn't talk with Sam much about what was coming at all. I felt a familiar rise in stress-levels but put this down to my three-month-old relationship becoming more serious; my partner and I had been talking not just of living together but moving. Sam said we could work on this but I wanted our remaining weeks together to be about just us.

I was adamant I'd go through with my plan. I wasn't aware of anything else to do differently to make leaving easier.

'Here's the bind: you won't know how I am afterwards. I can't both finish and then tell you.'

July 2004: I set the date for our final session, just two weeks ahead. This had to be the best way to keep dread to a minimum, like a dentist appointment or going back to school.

August 2nd 2004: Sam and I sat back against cushions, shoulder-to-shoulder. I checked my breathing: calm. I checked my thoughts: none, really. I was simply here, making the most of my final visit, sucking the last cuddle dry – it had to last a long, long time. I gazed at the far wall. Checked the clock. Fifteen whole minutes left. If I kept quite still and we didn't say a word, it'd go more slowly.

'It's time.' Who said those words, Sam or me? We stood up, shoulders separating. I glanced around the room. My shells were still on the windowsill. I had asked for them to stay there. I crossed the space between us for a last hug. I reversed to the doorway and stood to look. Just at Sam now, the room a fuzzy background. He looked back. I knew this face, I could never forget it. Alive. Warm. Waiting. Quizzical. I turned, walked along the attic passage, past the loo and down the stairs.

'It's alright, we're still here, he's still there,' I whispered. My legs kept walking.

I sat in my car and stared at the dashboard. I turned the ignition and pulled away. I glanced up at Sam's window, forbidding myself to toot-toot as I usually did.

I drove home and did normal home things. I turned to what I knew from prep-school: counting days (that I'd survived), teddies, bread. None prevented me missing him, and missing him more as weeks passed. I keened for comfort, for mothering, and lost pound after pound not from starving but from living with a perpetually revved engine.

Pining grew stronger by the week, overtaking any level I'd known before. The realisation there was no going back sank in.

I simply wouldn't allow it. I continued to search for an answer to a growing dilemma: was my anguish about Sam (in which case I'd have to bear it), or my partner (in which case something was fundamentally awry)? How could I tell the difference? I loved this man I was now living with, I wanted to be with him, not leave him. I just didn't want to feel this way.

'Right: here I am, having left Sam; here I am, talking weddings. This is Spike's world, moving from safe-man to sex-man (I was six when my mother married my stepfather). No wonder the panic. No wonder the magnet to this precise timing: my body is remembering. Good, I've worked it out. Now what? I feel ill all the time. What if this knot in my stomach turns into cancer?'

* * *

I didn't work out that my terror expressed as 'I'm going to die and I can't stop it' was the simulate-death (Freeze) response to trauma. Hence, it didn't occur to me to yell 'help'.

* * *

What I didn't understand at all was a daily cycle I had no control over which started by waking in dread each morning. This lasted through the day and abruptly abated at six every evening. What was happening that wound me up and brought relief day after day? What was this telling me, who was telling?

Decision-making was impossible, especially the big one about getting married. I dug as deep as I knew to discover the relationship between these two extremes. I came up with a number of explanations but none had the effect I hoped for: a way out from being this way.

* * *

I was trying to make a life-changing decision without settling down to enquire deeply, and patiently, how I felt and let answers arise in their own time. I was racing ahead to know to escape not only the discomfort of not-knowing but to divert my feelings from Sam. Attempting to reach safety this way left me feeling extremely unsafe.

* * *

I didn't say much to my partner. I cried silently (well-practised after years in dormitories), took myself upstairs, wandered out into the garden. I knew I was relating to him 'as if' he was someone else; how could I explain this without hurting his feelings? (See Appendix, *Allies in Healing.*) Another bind.

* * *

Nor was I able to say, much more simply, that it was me being 'as if' I was my little-girl self.

* * *

There was only one person I wanted to tell. After three months, by which time I'd lost a stone and a half, I broke out of my self-imposed rule ('I can't finish and tell you how I am') and rang Sam's number. I didn't want to book an appointment. I just needed to know he hadn't moved house or hadn't died, and for him to know I hadn't. Over the years, I'd learned to stay connected between sessions and even during holidays. But how could I sustain this with no contact at all? Not a call, not a letter?

* * *

My phone call broke the spell, or in scientific terms, forged a new pathway. Six years' work in unlearning and relearning enabled me to take this mega-risk of doing something unthinkable as a child. Saying a little of how I was (not the full story but not pretending either) and hearing Sam's voice was enough to remind me I was an adult woman with adult resources and plenty of connections. I needed her badly.

In this act, I exchanged harshness with compassion – and was met by Sam's generosity.

* * *

Of course, one call wasn't enough. We started doing what I knew was unusual after therapy: we found a way of relating that wasn't work and wasn't no-contact. It relied on mutual trust: often I was left after a call or meeting (these were rare, a couple per year) with work to do scooping up distressed little ones who were strongly reminded of visits by my father and of school outings, but I could and did. This was no longer Sam's job.

CHAPTER SIX

AFTERMATH

Soon after I was married, extreme moods having settled down, I took myself back to therapy. I'd known for a while that one day I'd want to work with a woman. I searched carefully before making my choice.

2005/2007: 'I've come to work on endings.'

To her I brought my ongoing relationship with Sam. I feared her judgement: 'bad practice'; worse, 'bad therapy'; worse still, 'bad therapist'. I knew deep in my bones our relationship had been, and continued to be precious, invaluable; I'd defend that to the nth degree but still I wanted reassurance.

I was glad she didn't attempt to judge, either way. Little by little, I was coming to know better the voice which hovered on my right shoulder, claiming it as mine and listening more closely to the messages hiding beneath layers of defensive criticism.

2008: One moment in particular with Sam kept coming to mind (see Appendix, *Class, Prejudice & Privilege*), a moment I'd always known to be significant but hadn't followed to its resolution.

'Privileged?' The rest of my explosion had been a splutter. Just months into my first year of therapy I'd blundered through layers of apology and defiantly exposed myself as posh, including the family tradition of public school education. Although I realised that Sam's use of the 'P' word referred to having enough food and a roof over my head, I still heard an implied 'count yourself lucky'.

'You'll be my expert in these matters,' he'd said later when my indignation had subsided. Once more, I'd swelled with pride and took it upon myself to outline many *'Poshland'* customs. But I didn't get to filling in the details of both physical and emotional deprivation of boarding school or the wrenching goodbyes. I had had plenty of other things, and people, to rant about, plenty of work to be going on with.

I reflected back on my entire process of leaving Sam and saw replication everywhere: from minimal preparation, not talking about it (to talk made it real which in turn risked feeling), re-signed tramping away with no going back, to getting used to it, digging in to endure (see Appendix, *The Making of Them*). This, and more, I recognised.

At last I had another handle on my panic and pining and someone to tell, both about our ending and about school.

What came to me a lot more slowly was that in part I blamed him, enough to prevent our work from feeling truly finished. Why hadn't he stopped me leaving in the manner I had?

How good this was to realise, albeit scary. How could I reconcile the Sam I loved with the Sam who hadn't been perfect for me in every respect? Who hadn't rescued me when I'd been little (even though he'd said he would have done if he'd been there, even though we did recreate scenes of 'being found and rescued' in the therapy room)? Who hadn't done something to make finishing less painful for me?

No wonder I'd pushed fear (of what all this meant) out onto my shoulder, in the guise of Judge-Critic. No wonder I'd tried to project judgements onto my current therapist. I was determined to thrash my way through this one, for the sake of all endings.

A memory returned of Sam once saying, 'I'm really sorry you're feeling so bad, but I'm absolutely not sorry for what I did.' (This had been his response to my attempt at blaming him for a moment when I'd been scared by his angry retort – to an insult I'd delivered.) I imagined him saying this again now; he hadn't been and still wasn't responsible for my choices, however sorry he might feel towards how I was hurting.

Responsibility. This was where I was heading. I'd believed for a long time that blaming had to be gone through rather than by-passed. I still did; I realised I'd been so deeply immersed no part of me had been available to notice. First step, recognition.

Blame, self-blame included, had been a mental exercise of trying to work out 'who's fault?' About everything. Rage, blame, collapse, guilt, despair, try-to-make-it-alright-reasoning, stale-mate, despair, rage... round and round going nowhere, my body locked in frustration to protect me from feeling everything else.

* * *

Realising brought me one step closer to the word I reviled most – acceptance. Got to accept, let go, move on? Who said?

* * *

Another thought: if I could reconcile my feelings towards Sam, might I have a template for reconciling my feelings towards my mother? It seemed a big leap, but...

Next, my tutors' words came to me, this time about separating being and doing, the distinction between person and behaviour.

* * *

Reconciling my feelings inside me – that was the bridge. And crossing slowly, step at a time. No leaping.

The urge to escape the present had been my lifetime's habit. Side-effect? Missing whatever was happening right now. Well, that had been the original point, to not-feel. Hadn't I missed enough? Did I want to carry on missing my life? Wouldn't I get to the end and wish I'd been in myself more, missed less?

My realisation opened the door. To step through required more.

* * *

2009: The title of a talk, 'Trauma of the Privileged Child' spoke directly to my nine year-old heart. Encouraged, I felt brave enough to enrol in group therapy work with Boarding Concern (see Appendix).

When the therapists there talked of self-betrayal, my system baulked. How dare they imply I'd betrayed myself as a child, it was others who'd betrayed me.

Only when I breathed out could I sense there was something here worth listening to. Ok, so when I was little I did start ignoring how I felt and stifling protest, taking up pretending instead, ('How are you?' 'I'm fine'). Clever me, clever survival instinct, a form of the Freeze response to being trapped with no escape from what was happening at home or from the regime at school. Responsible for this course of action? Here was the tangle. I understood the bit about being responsible for recovery; was I being asked to take responsibility for what had happened that I'd had no control over? Didn't that let 'them' off the hook whoever 'they' were? Round I went again, refusing to accept an idea so outrageous.

Years before I'd written an article, *The Power of Remorse* (see Appendix, *Self & Society*), trying to grapple with the concept of forgiveness which had always been a sticking point for me. Just as saying 'sorry' had to come freely given from the heart if it was to mean anything, surely 'that's alright' had to be just the same, not an attempt, excuses included, to avoid the issue of what had happened and who was responsible.

This was big, I knew. Stay with it, breathe, slow down, let it come...

Got it: shine the light away from 'them' and 'what they did' and onto my experience, my feelings. Was this what these therapists meant?

I smiled. The smile filled my stomach. 'Told you,' sang my little girl inside. I took her hand. She'd known all along 'it's what happens afterwards that matters most'. In poured my sorry, to myself, and no question that this was heartfelt. 'I'm sorry that things I did, for me, cost so much, to me.' I felt my chest move as stubborn refusal gave way, felt myself opening, felt warmth spreading through.

* * *

Saying and hearing my 'sorry' (no forcing, no 'you've got to move on') was another moment of moving back in, welcoming all who I had been, including actions I had taken.

My recurring childhood nightmare made sense at last: being chased up a narrow path by something terrifying, me straining to run through glue, barely moving, it closing in, me waking in terror just before being grabbed.

As my first tutor had intimated years back, when I was ready and able to turn round I'd find not an ogre nor my stepfather but me behind me – the part which had been split off but refused to be left behind: the feelings part.

* * *

Of course I hesitated at the prospect of exchanging longing for registering loss – for Sam, for my children, for my mother when I'd needed her, for my father when I'd needed him: loss for connections that mattered most. Beseeching the outside world to make things different, and raging when it didn't, was so familiar. So was guilt. Loss meant staying put, living in my body, not escaping, meant feeling sad; meant, above all, accepting.

Could I learn to live not-knowing what might happen next, dare I loosen my hold? Could I 'let go' of the expectation of being left, of being shamed, of coping alone? Could I complete my welcome of the banished schoolgirl (unlike all the other me's, she had no name) to whom goodbye had meant waiting and enduring, no end in sight.

This was a matter of trust, then, that whatever happened from now on something fundamental would be different. What could that be? Ah… an adult present, one with sole intent of taking care of me. Myself.

Then, and only then, did I realise there was yet one more piece missing. *Anger.* Not frustrated blame-rage, more than spurts of protest – straight clear outrage on my behalf.

The biggest one of all. I was ready: *I needed my own adult outrage for my little-girl self.* My 'hey, that wasn't alright' protest expressed by my younger selves over and over again, starting in Sam's barn, was badly needed by all of them from me too: adult anger and protection (Fight/Flight energy) was what had been missing. I needed to make and hear my adult response, my own 'lioness' roar'.

My now-therapist persistently reminded and encouraged me to slow down, to listen to my body, to allow this energy to emerge: any coercion and my system clenched tight back into 'won't, can't'. I committed once again to patience, to day-by-day paying attention.

As I worked, I felt blame and criticism falling away, of Sam first and then of myself. And if I didn't blame, I needn't defend, excuse or explain. I could live with what was. Fight-energy needed for this form of self-acceptance felt very different from rage: muscles warm and limbered up rather than solid and sore. My back was straightening, I found myself looking out rather than down. Feeling rather than defending against the pain of how I left Sam encouraged me; I was coming closer to accepting the most painful decisions of all, to feeling the deepest losses.

Not alone, that was for sure. And not all at once, but slowly and with self-compassion, so I neither defended nor crumbled.

* * *

2010: Returning to my body frees me from the prison of raging against what cannot be changed; at the heart of this lies the inescapable truth that I do not exist in isolation and do not thrive if I try to – no wonder I'd felt homesick and wondered what was missing. And releases energy to work towards what can be.

Living in my adult self as I *am* frees me to know Sam as he *is* (no longer as 'brother, lover, father, mother'). Frees me to relate as I am now to my mother as she is now. And so on. The equation is simple: the less I judge myself, the less I relate defensively to others; the more I honour my story, the more receptive I can be to theirs.

Here I am, at border control. I've shown my passport, the barrier is up. Before stepping through, I take time for one last look round. I breathe out and say 'Goodbye', out loud, to Sam.

CONCLUSION

There is, then, no 'great escape' from the behaviours and patterns we most desire to change. Many relationships, connections and activities can be therapeutic and valuable but are not 'therapy' per se. Whatever the variety of therapy offered, the essential components are the same: a relationship between two parties (however many individuals make up either one) formed with the explicit dynamic of client and therapist to work together, the quality of which depends on quality of attention paid to each part.

Individually, each experience of therapy is bound to be unique since neither client nor therapist, and hence the relationship, is exactly like any other. My story demonstrates how therapy *can* work. If any readers wondering whether therapy might work for them are thinking, 'I don't want to do what she did,' my reply is, 'Good, it wouldn't be possible, my story cannot be yours.' If any are thinking, 'I want what she had with Sam,' my reply is, 'Good; my story can be like a map to help identify what you might need, to fold up once you get going.'

Just as a client makes his initial call at a particular stage in his life, so the therapist who responds will be at hers. Her experience is not the issue; her commitment to ethical practice, including ongoing self-enquiry and peer consultation (supervision), is.

When I knocked on Sam's door the first time, I was seeking a sense of belonging rather than meaning, which I didn't even understand as a concept. My desire to belong, together with persistent curiosity, has however brought me gifts of meaning that keep on coming, even as I write: the more I belong to myself, the more I can choose which packs to belong to and so explore the world beyond; and the more I feel safe enough to face and live rather than run from my experiences.

'I wish I'd known this sooner,' I mutter. My wish tells me I'm going too fast; I change to a lower gear.

'You don't have to do it all at once,' I hear Sam's voice reminding me.

I add to that, 'And 'moving on' doesn't mean leaving my past behind; I bring it (me) along as my personal maintenance manual.'

I spent another six years completing my work with Sam, learning, learning, finding my way to becoming adult – with help from my own, female, kind. Ending has included acknowledging and accepting that Sam was first and foremost my therapist. ('How can I say goodbye fully if I haven't fully said hello?') Everything more we became grew from him being himself rather than withholding, from receiving and treasuring my gift of little-girl love during what I've come to know as my 'second childhood' – for which I am ever grateful.

Healing from trauma is likely to leave some parts more vulnerable than others that might always need special attention. Saying 'goodbye' is my 'Achilles heel'. Living my goodbyes is what I returned to therapy to learn.

How can I know what I need and make choices as to what action to take if I don't take time and trouble to inquire how I feel? If I don't pay attention to clues of distress such as busyness and racing ahead? Nobody and nothing 'makes me' angry or sad or afraid or happy. My feelings, emotional and physical, are nature's way of providing me with information. Isn't welcoming and responding to them the essence of taking care?

* * *

I'm up-to-date. It's time to draw in threads and bring my narrative to a close. If you're wondering what happened to Fairytale Cottage, the stories Sam and I made up dried up naturally as focus shifted and needs changed, as did writing rhymes. As for my family of bears, I did buy a mother-bear but she didn't come to the therapy room. They all sit together on a shelf, there if I need them as reminder.

I've discovered from reading more widely that what I've written about 'Autonomous Dependence' is another exposition of enquiry about humanity that began with the earliest philosophers (before science and art became separate). I've attempted to link my own thinking to a wider, collective wondering – driven by curiosity rather than need for definitive answers.

As to the original question, it has prompted me to investigate places, both deep inside and far out into the world, I couldn't have anticipated when I began; and feel feelings I didn't know were in me. Which replicates exactly my experience of therapy.

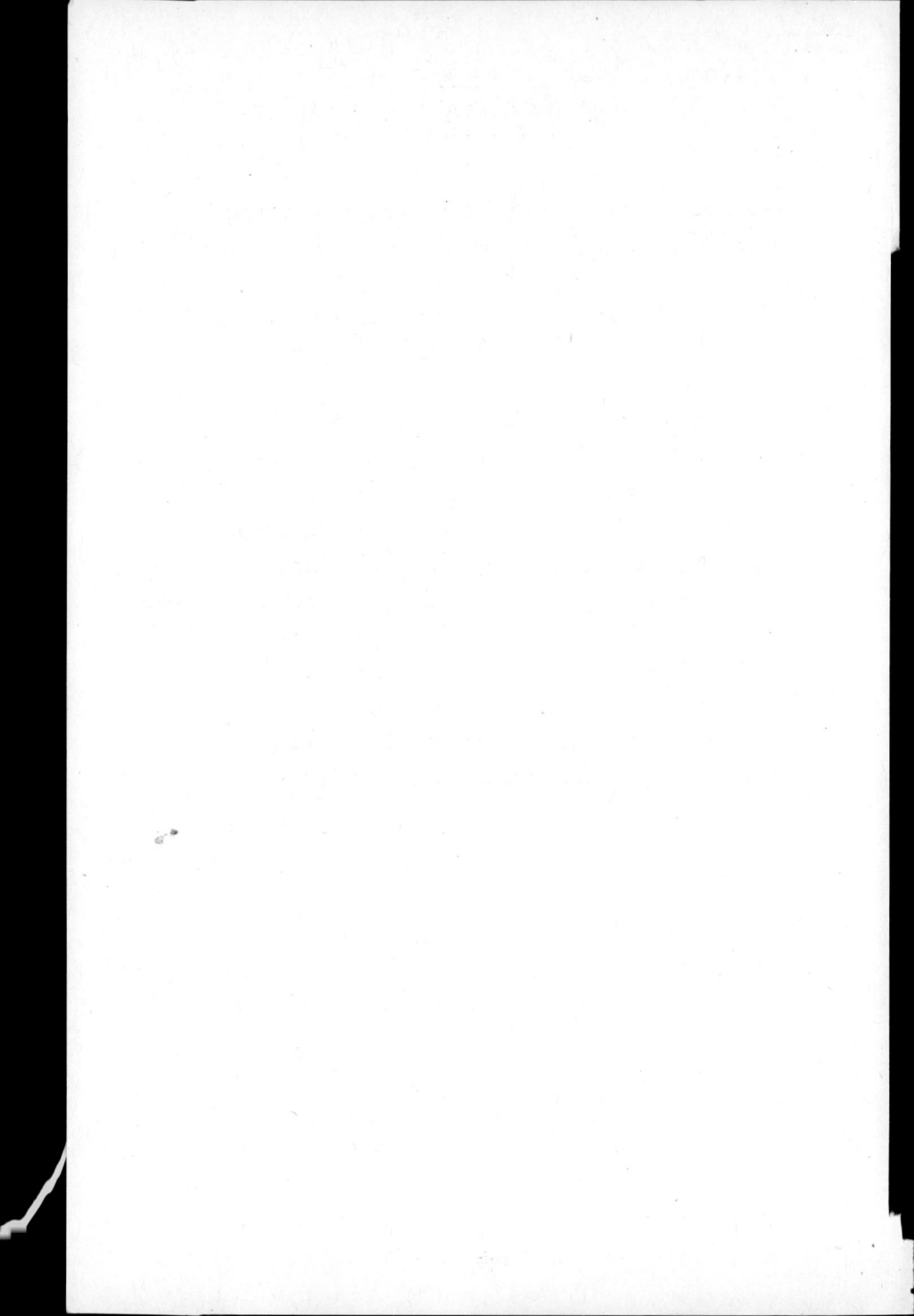

CODA

I wrote this in 1996 at the end of my first year's training. The title was, 'The role of the counsellor'.

It's ok to be angry, it's ok to be sad,
It's ok to feel frightened, I don't need to pretend,
It's ok to be silent, to sit here and cry,
You stay with me, quietly, and don't ask me why.

Layer by layer you help me dig down
Freeing truths half-forgotten, not admitted, not known,
No shock, disapproval, no scorn, no blame,
You accept who I am, my guilt and my shame.

No tidy solutions, advice, sorting out,
The choices are mine, for me to decide
To stay bitter and hurt, stay ruled by my past,
Or break free to enjoy being me at last.

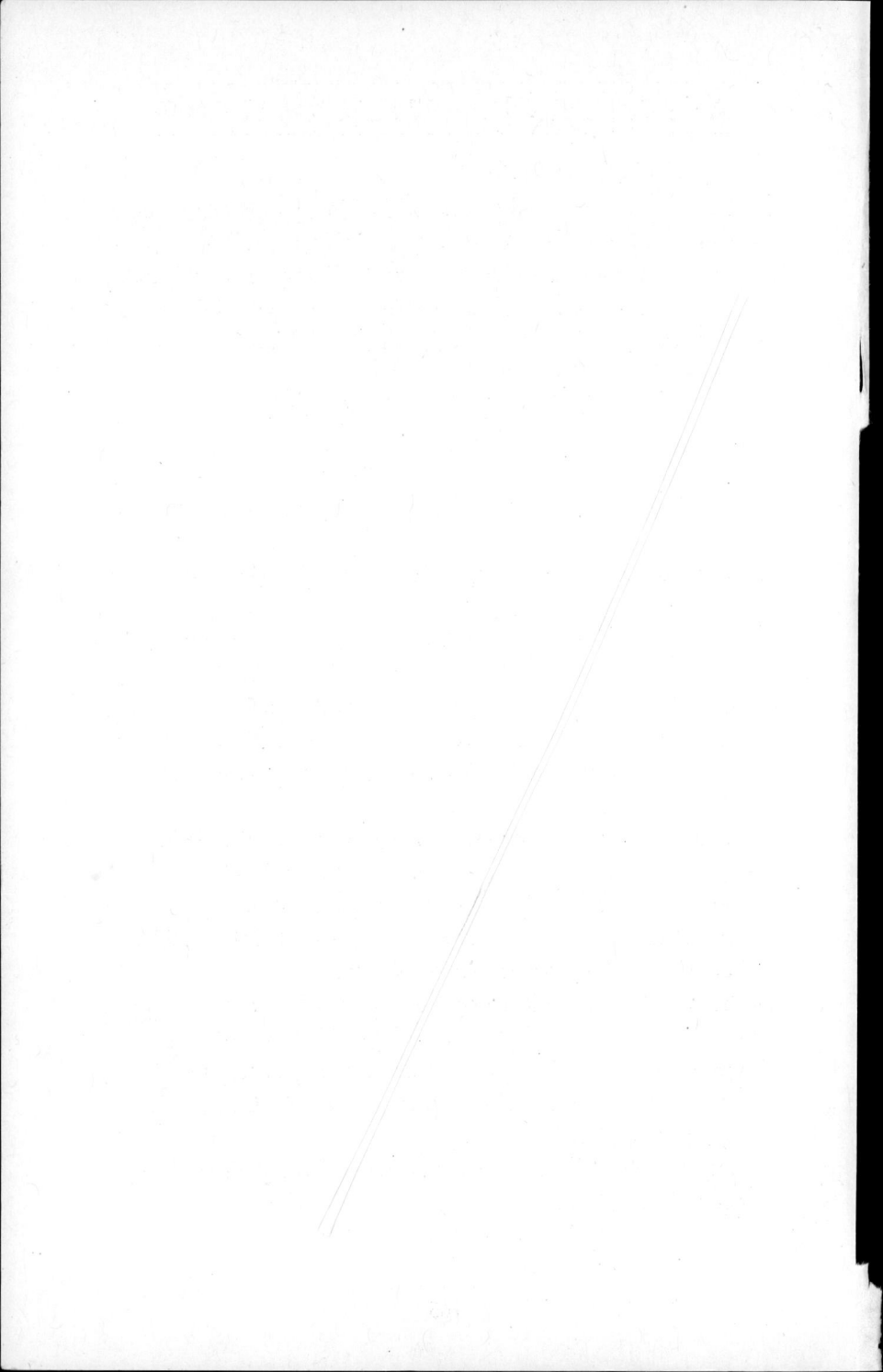

APPENDIX: FURTHER READING

Axline, Virginia — *Dibs, In Search of Self:* Penguin Books, 1964.

Barclay, Jane — *Class, Prejudice and Privilege:* Self & Society, Journal for Association for Humanistic Psychology in Britain (Vol. 30, no 4), *The Power of Remorse:* Self & Society (Vol. 31, no 2), *Sacrifice:* Self & Society (Vol. 32, no 4), *'I can't get no-o... Satisfaction':* Self & Society (Vol. 34, no5).

Barclay, Jane — *The Trauma of Boarding at School:* www.boardingconcern.org.uk

Barker, Pat — *Regeneration:* Viking, 1991.

Batmanghelidjh, Camila — *Shattered Lives:* Jessica Kingsley Publishers, 2006.

Bowlby, John — *The Making and Breaking of Affectional Bonds:* Tavistock Publications, 1979.

Coveney, Peter — *The Image of Childhood:* Peregrine Books, 1967.

Davies, Laura — *Allies in Healing:* HarperCollins, 1991.

Duffel, Nick — *The Making of Them:* Lone Arrow Press, 2000.

Gerhardt, Sue — *Why Love Matters:* Routledge, 2004

Greenfield, Susan — *The Private Life of the Brain:* Penguin Books, 2000.

Herman, Judith — *Trauma and Recovery:* HarperCollins, 1992.

Laing, R. D. — *The Divided Self:* Penguin Books, 1960.

LeDoux, J — *The Emotional Brain:* Phoenix, 1999.

Levine, Peter — *Waking the Tiger:* North Atlantic Books, 1997.

Miller, Alice — *Banished Knowledge:* Virago, 1991.

Rothschild, Babette — *The Body Remembers:* Norton, 2000.

Rothschild, Babette — *Help for the Helper:* Norton, 2006.

Rutter, Peter — *Sex in the Forbidden Zone:* Jeremy P. Tarcher, 1989.

Winnicott, D. W. — *The Child, the Family, and the Outside World:* Penguin Books, 1964.

Yalom, Irvine — *Love's Executioner and Other Tales of Psychotherapy:* Penguin Books, 1991.